Marrisa

I Thank You!

Paul Wayne

Unremembered *Wings*

One Orphanage, Two Angels,
and a Lost Boy Finding
Unconditional Love

PAUL WAYNE

Unremembered Wings: One Orphanage, Two Angels,
and a Lost Boy Finding Unconditional Love
by Paul Wayne

© 2012 Paul Wayne

Cover art: "The Angels" by Deborah Bridges, used with permission. www.studiobridges.com.

Writing and editorial assistance: Faith Marcovecchio, Mark Graham Communications, www.markgrahamcommunications.com

Book design by Nick Zelinger, www.nzgraphics.com

Author photo (on jacket) by Katie Andelman, www.katieandelman.com

ISBN (Hard Cover): 978-0-9857822-1-4
ISBN (Soft Cover): 978-0-9857822-0-7

Library of Congress Control Number: Pending

First Edition

Printed in the United States of America

This book is dedicated to Sister Janice Buescher
and Sister Ellen Babin, in honor and recognition
for a lifetime of unwavering devotion,
relentless service, and unconditional love.

" …and something ignited my soul,
fever or unremembered wings.
and I went my own way
deciphering that burning fire,
and suddenly I saw the heavens
unfastened and open."

~ Pablo Neruda

Contents

Preface

It was late on a beautiful Sunday morning in the Pacific Northwest, and I wasn't going to let the day pass me by. Groggy and needing some stand-in energy, I threw my legs over the side of the bed, stood, and rubbed my eyes. Still tired. Twenty-four-hour call at the hospital the night before had left me sitting on empty, and I needed coffee, bad.

Fortunately, heavy doses of caffeine were just a few steps away. Energized by Starbucks and a warm shower, I turned to the day's plans: an afternoon in Edmonds on Puget Sound to take in the town's yearly arts and crafts festival. I wasn't about to let my long shift in the obstetrics wing usurp my plans.

I kept my expectations simmering on low. A lot of art isn't particularly creative or new, especially at an art show, but I knew the combination of fresh air, visual stimulation, and perhaps a nice glass of Washington state wine would make the drive worth my while. As I circulated through the aisles, I felt the hazy fog lift from my brain and the energy of the day creep in.

Suddenly, I turned the corner, and there they were. Two exquisitely beautiful angels, a pair of statues titled "Unremembered Wings."

One taller, the other shorter; I couldn't help but be reminded of two women I knew well, the nuns I considered my parents. I spent two hours with the artist, telling her my story, sharing my connection to those women—both real and represented in her art—and talking about the writing they inspired in me. Deborah Bridges, the sculptor, was inspired by writing too, in her case the poetry of Pablo Neruda. An excerpt from his work accompanied the statues.

It seemed more than coincidental that this sculpture and Neruda's words resonated so deeply with me. I had recently begun working on a book that combined my own poetry with my story as a child growing up in an orphanage, a story centered on two women I considered angels in my own life. With Deborah's permission, I planned to name the book after her statues, and I hoped my work would be as inspiring to others as hers was to me.

The two women who quietly helped me and dozens of other children find love and acceptance never asked for attention or rewards for their work. They did it humbly, in service to God. They did it on unremembered wings. This is our story.

Preface

Flawed

I stood there,
Kicked in the stomach,
I stood there,
Gasping for Oxygen,
I stood there,
Unable to Breathe, unable to move,
I cried there,
Shaking, lonely, and suddenly empty,
I cried there,
Holding my too young sister,
I cried there,
Holding my too young brother,
I sat there,
Chest quivering, lost,
I sat there,
Grasping security, grasping air, grasping hands.

What had I done…

CHAPTER 1

"Yes, Sir"

"We're going for a ride. Get in the truck."

Phillip, Tina, and I looked at each other apprehensively. When did we ever go for a joyride with Dad? Never. But we all knew one thing: when he told us to do something, there was only one right answer, "Yes, sir." Either that, or get ready for a whipping.

We climbed into the faded green pickup, our little butts and scrawny knees scrunched side by side on the wide bench seat. Except for the faint hum of the road beneath us and the soft sound of country songs coming from the radio, we sat in silence. At nine and eight, Phil and I could read the green-and-white road signs well enough to know we were headed for Houma. As for Tina, even if she'd been big enough to see out the window, her five-year-old eyes wouldn't have been able to make sense of the letters.

Houma was only twenty minutes from the crappy subdivision where we lived, but it sure felt farther that day. Finally, the truck turned onto a white oyster-shell-lined driveway canopied by magnificent live oaks, their arms brushing against the sky. I looked for a sign—nothing. But soon the white buildings set on sweeping green lawns told me all I needed to know. Sure enough, when I craned my neck I could see them: girls and boys, playing and staring back at me through the tall, wood-framed windows.

Two minutes later, and Dad's Chevy screeched to a halt at the end of the circular drive. Phil's frightened eyes caught mine. They said what the twinges in my stomach were already telling me. *This can't be good.* A sharp bark from my father confirmed it:

"Get out."

In my mind's eye I can still see the gray concrete steps, the massive wooden doors, the three skinny, raggedy kids trailing behind their determined, angry father. Inside, a lady offered us water and a place to sit, then cake, obviously left over from some earlier event. "What kind is it?" I asked, hoping through my anxiety that I might see something good out of this day after all. "Shut up. You're rude," my dad snapped back. Head down, I nodded, and the three of us sat, quietly holding hands, Phillip to my left and Tina to my right.

Dad spoke to a woman at a desk, then hunched over a table, signing paperwork. Looking back, I'll never forget how matter-of-fact it all was, like he was filling out a deposit slip at the bank. In minutes, it was done.

I watched him as he stood and, with an audible exhale of relief, stepped quickly to the door. This was it. His hand was on the tarnished gold knob. I leapt to my feet.

"No," he said darkly, his lifeless eyes barely turning to look at us. "You're not coming with me."

And abruptly, he vanished through the crackled white doors.

* * *

It was the spring of 1974 the day my father dropped us off at MacDonell Methodist Children's Home in Houma, Louisiana, less than 30 miles from the trailer where he and my stepmother lived. Little did we know it would be years before we saw him again. All we had were the clothes on our backs—no suitcases, no toys or books, not even a change of underwear. In the days before we took that one-way car ride and in the years that followed, Simon Buras Sr. never explained his decision to leave us, his three youngest kids, at the local orphanage and calmly drive away. Like a lot of things, he kept that to himself.

As the sound of the truck's tires faded into the distance, my brother, sister, and I sat a little longer, taking it all in. The lady who had offered us cake and showed Dad where to sign each page of our intake papers watched silently for a moment. Then, with kindness in her eyes, she came out from behind her desk and told us gently that it was time to go to our cottages. Feeling cold and distant, I got up and followed her out the door and across the lawn, Tina and Phillip in my wake. We had begun our journey, away from everything we'd ever known and into our new lives.

* * *

In the back, in the way back, there had been five of us: Simon Jr., Tommy, Phillip, me, and Tina. I was the youngest boy at six; my oldest brother was fourteen. That day we were all there, watching Simon Sr. beat the holy crap out of our mom. It was far from the first time, but the two oldest boys decided that it would be the last.

Young Simon and Tommy both got shotguns for Christmas that year. While Dad continued to rage unstopped, they headed for their room. Dad must not have heard Simon load the gun's chamber, because he looked surprised to feel the cool metal barrel pressed against his forehead. His fist was still clenched, preparing for another blow.

"You hit her one more time, and I'll kill you," Simon said quietly.

Tommy had him covered from behind. All I could do was watch and cry.

"Is this how you want it?" Dad bellowed.

"I'll shoot you right now," Simon replied calmly. "You can't hit her again."

And that's how it worked out—Dad's raised fist slowly opened and fell to his side. He walked out that night, and it was only a matter of time before he filed for divorce. None of us thought we'd never see him again. For better or worse, we were on our own.

* * *

Walking down the long sidewalk from MacDonell's administration building, our first stop was Keener, the cottage for the younger girls. Next we headed to Hooper. From the outside, the building was plain, brick, single story. Inside, the space was divided into two main living areas, a dining room and a living room combo on the left, with a small reading and play area on the right. A long tile-covered hallway led to the bedrooms, and seemed very dark at the end.

My room was simple, clean, bare. An empty single bed and desk sat on one side; the same setup, only occupied, sat on the other. Each half of the room had a built-in closet. That was it. This was home.

Though Phil and I would live in the same cottage, each of us had our own rooms, our own roommates. Mine was also named Paul, later to be called "Z," whereas I'd be "B." Phil would be Phil, quiet, fearful, and a loner, same as he'd been his whole life.

* * *

After Dad left the night of the beating, times got lean. A meal I could count on most of the time was mayonnaise on bread, my favorite sandwich. Mom would disappear for days or weeks, then show up with some groceries before heading out again. Where she went, none of us knew. Houston was a big place, and our little house in Splendora, filled with five rambunctious kids, must have felt small.

It wasn't too long before the neighbors started to notice. Five kids, no adult supervision: it wasn't hard to figure out. A year or so in, someone called the Department of Human Services. DHS didn't have much of a choice but to take us into custody. Because of their ages, Simon and Tommy were given the choice to stay.

DHS tracked Dad down. Put Phil, Tina, and me on a bus with my oldest brother Simon serving as the court-appointed chaperone. The few clothes we had we stuffed into grocery bags. And that's how our father found us at the bus station: three scared kids holding brown paper sacks, our last memory of him beating our mother while Simon Jr. held a shotgun to his head. Welcome to southern Louisiana.

* * *

Bom, bom, bom. A wrought iron bell rang in the distance. Settled in as much as we could be with nothing to unpack, Phil and I followed the lead of the eight other boys in our cottage and filed over to the dining hall for dinner.

Kids poured out of three other buildings nearby. I watched closely, sizing them up. Black kids, Indians, white kids, and a bunch I wasn't sure about. Boys and girls. Some who looked big enough to be in high school, others as young as Tina. Each cottage contained eight or ten children, so there must have been thirty-five, forty in all. Plus the adult counselors, who led each group.

Despite my nerves, I was hungry. It'd been a while since my last meal. The smell of a good dinner with meat and vegetables and rice greeted us as we sat down at long tables set with silverware and napkins. Pretty soon, one of the older kids from our table put a plate of food in front of each of us and we said grace. Quietly, still watching the others, I began to eat. The sound of chatter and joking filled the room. In it, I could feel the cadence of comfortable routine. Ever so slightly, I let it seep in.

"Yes, Sir"

A Gift

a gift of life,
a gift to serve,
a gift of humility,
a gift to smile,
a gift of awareness,
a gift to embrace those who hurt,
a gift of sharing,
a gift to give hope in darkness,
a gift of warmth in loneliness,
a gift to care when you're forgotten,
a gift of appreciation,
a gift to Love those closest to You,

a gift is Giving, Living, and Loving!

my gifts,
your gifts,

remember your gifts.

CHAPTER 2

Holding Up
a Mirror

That fall I started fourth grade in the Terrebonne Parish School District. It was reassuring to know I wasn't going to a new school alone. There were lots of other kids from the home who caught the bus at the back gate of MacDonell's. The rest, like my sister Tina, stayed on campus because they needed the extra help.

In some ways, it was a relief to be back in school. I could be my old self in class, the talkative clown, without worrying about everyone knowing my father and stepmother had dumped me in an orphanage. I never told anyone where I lived. And I blended in fine. I was smart, good at sports. We'd been given plenty of decent clothes from the hand-me-down room on campus. And on top of that, I knew how to defend myself if anyone tried to bully me or Phil.

That came in handy at MacDonell's, because if you didn't watch out you could get your ass whipped just about every day—especially if you were the new kid. You had to learn how to roll with it or it rolled you. I was not one to be rolled, and so I got into a few fights. Simon Jr. and Tommy had taught me how to protect myself by beating me up regularly back in Splendora.

Phil and Tina needed me to watch out for them, too. The bigger, more physically dominating guys at MacDonell's, like

21

Albert Jones, would intentionally tickle my sister or hit or slap her just to provoke me. And Phil would never, ever defend himself physically—or even verbally. He couldn't do it, and so he was a kid that bullies loved to pick on, at school and at the orphanage. Because of that I fought, and set a precedent that you didn't mess with me or my family.

But even while I was elbowing my way into MacDonell's pecking order, I knew I was in a safe place. None of the adults yelled at me or physically hurt me. I could count on dinner at five, a nice playground to run around on after school, and a dependable pillow to sleep on at night. My new roommate Z and I got along great. We made our room come alive with posters and pictures cut out from magazines, and kept it as clean as two eight-year-olds could. I'd made other friends too, like Sarah, a girl my age who lived in Keener. The counselor who lived in our cottage fixed us breakfast in the morning and a snack when we got home from school, and joined us for endless games of softball, flag football, and tag on the weekends. Sundays we went to church. My life began to have structure. With relief, I embraced it. But what gave me the greatest sense of constancy at MacDonell's was Sister Janice.

* * *

I'd never met a nun before Sister Janice. At first, I didn't know what to make of her. She was tall, imposing. Solid. And she wore a habit, something I'd never seen before.

She came to the orphanage as school administrator, and from her first day, no matter where you went, she always seemed to be around. Sitting with us at dinner. Checking in on the kids' ceramics classes. Meeting with the counselors and social workers. Heading back to her house on campus each night.

There was something about her that let you know things were under control, that she had it covered. Even though pretty much every one of us kids had come from violence, chaos, unreliable parents and unhappy homes, we knew that while we were at MacDonell's, Sister Janice was going to take good care of us. Silently, with her day-to-day actions, she told us we mattered.

* * *

One night, early on after Sister Janice arrived, I woke up to the sound of banging against my wall. Not little taps, loud pounding sounds that made the wall shake. I got up to take a look around.

In the next room, my cottage mate James was going nuts. Jumping off the bed, kicking the walls, yelling and cussing at whoever would listen. Sister Janice sat in a chair next to the door. She had a book and was reading it, calm as could be. No matter how wild James got, she didn't look up. When she saw me, she told me to go back to bed, then returned to her book. Eventually, I heard the sounds of James's violence fade away. She let him get his demons out while she quietly sat there, seeing him through his pain.

That was her gift. She had a mirror, and she held it up for you every second of the day, allowing you to see yourself clearly and decide who you wanted to be.

* * *

23

It was something I really needed. By the time I got to junior high I had become the official class clown, constantly goofing around and getting into trouble. Part of the problem was that school was just not challenging enough for me; in Louisiana, where poverty rates were high and test scores were low, I felt like I was just jumping through hoops until I could get back out to recess and have some fun.

Eventually, teachers from my various classes got fed up with me and sent me down to the principal's office. There, if the transgression was serious enough, Miss Jackson would give you a choice: a paddling or a phone call to your mother—which in my case was Sister Janice. I played it safe and always took the paddle.

The principal's weapon of choice was as long as a baseball bat with one side shaved off into a wide, flat surface. She'd have you take the position—bent over her big wooden desk with your hands resting on the top—then give you three good, hard smacks on the butt. It hurt like holy hell. The one consolation was that I could keep my punishment to myself.

After you'd taken your licks, Miss Jackson would send you out into the hallway. She'd say, "Now go out there and sit down, and when I'm ready to deal with you I'll come out and talk to you." Waiting was part of the punishment. When it came to psychological warfare, Miss Jackson was nobody's fool.

One day, after three especially hard whacks, I sat in the hallway, rocking back and forth to distract myself from my stinging butt. Suddenly, I could feel someone standing over me. I looked up, and cringed to discover it was Sister Janice. Even though she was there on account of another kid from

MacDonell's, it didn't take long for her to put together what I'd been up to. I was busted.

Punishment at the home was different from what I'd experienced with my parents or my alcoholic stepmother. No one screamed at you, threw things, said you were worthless, slapped you in the face. Instead, you were held accountable by having the things you loved the most taken away. Like riding your bike? Sorry, no bike privileges. Can't wait to get home from school to play basketball? Guess you'll be sitting on the bench. And don't even think about going fishing or crabbing with Sister Ellen, who was in charge of recreation.

At first it all seemed unfair, but eventually you gained perspective and learned about consequences. Especially if you had to meet with Sister Janice before the consequences were set. She never accused you of bad behavior. She helped you think it through.

One day, after screwing around in English class, I took the bus home and headed for Laskey, the older boys' cottage. Instead of handing me an after-school snack, my counselor told me that Sister Janice wanted to see me in her office.

Crap.

English was already history in my mind, so all the way over to the administration building I debated what I'd done wrong. When I finally got to Sister Janice's office, she was sitting behind her desk, going through a stack of paperwork. "Sit down," she told me. "Let's talk."

While she continued working, she presented me with a scenario. "Now what if you ran across a kid or someone else who was making funny noises constantly, for no apparent reason? What would you think about that?"

"Well," I said slowly, "I'd wonder what's going on with him. Is he weird? Why is he making the noises? Can't he hear himself?"

"Right," she said. "I'd wonder that too."

She paused for a while, signed a few more forms.

"Now, I got a call from your teacher today about someone making all these noises and acting up in the back of her class. Do you know anything about that?" she finally said.

Oh. Suddenly, maybe for the first time, I saw myself through other people's eyes. I had to account for my behavior and own it. Normally, I would have denied what I'd done or made an excuse. Instead, in a calming way Sister Janice helped me think about my behavior objectively. I didn't get into any trouble. I just realized with surprise that I didn't see myself like everyone else saw me.

She was holding up a mirror.

* * *

I moved from Hooper to Laskey the fall I turned ten. By then, Tina, Phil, and I had lived at MacDonell's for two years. We never left campus to go home, not even on Christmas, when most of the other kids went to their parents' for the holidays. Some of the full-timers tried to fool themselves by packing a suitcase and waiting by the door, but not us. We knew no one was coming.

Right around that time, Phil decided to move back to Texas to live with our mom. It was where he wanted to be, even though there wasn't much there for any of us. I think he just needed the quiet of our old empty house, and so he petitioned the state to send him back. Me, I knew better than that. My gut instinct told me MacDonell's was a heck of a lot better place to grow up than Splendora, even if you did have to fight off a few bullies. But deep down I also knew Phil and I were different, and needed different things. He would never have the coping skills I did. So while I moved over to Laskey, he moved out of our lives.

Even though I'd been admiring the older boys for years, when it finally came time to join them in their cottage, it felt like it had happened overnight. Not only would I be living with them, I'd be sitting at their table in the dining room, playing beside them on the football field, and overseeing the little kids on field trips and during chores.

There was an unspoken power structure at MacDonell's owing to the physical size of the big kids and how they related to everyone else on campus. Some, like Poncho, took the time to play with us littler boys, teaching us how to throw a football, hit a softball, or toss a Frisbee. He was our elder statesman: soft-spoken, polite, hard-working, and considerate. Others, like Albert, were intimidating, ultra-aggressive, and into bragging that they were headed off to prison someday just like their daddies. Now I was about to join their ranks.

Moving day felt like Christmas Eve—my stomach was full of butterflies. I borrowed a red wagon and piled my stuff up in the bed. The whole way down the narrow, cracked sidewalk from Hooper, I danced and juggled to keep anything from falling out. Behind me my old Ranger Rick animal posters were stuffed in the trash, the room Z and I shared swept clean and polished until it shone.

In my new room in Laskey, it took several hours to get everything ordered just like I liked it. I made sure every hanger hung exactly one inch apart in the closet, measuring the distance with my trusty wooden ruler. Shirts had to be on the left and dress pants on the right, with my three pairs of shoes down below, lined up perfectly side by side with the shoelaces tucked in. The chest of drawers was also methodically arranged by color, size, and clothing type.

In addition to wanting high scores for neatness, and therefore a better allowance, I found comfort in order and hierarchy. It was the way I organized my life.

* * *

There was, however, one part to my structured routine that I couldn't stand: talking to the social worker.

Every week at the home, each kid had to meet with a therapist to talk about their past, their family, what was going on in school, with the other kids at MacDonell's, with their parents if they went home. An hour a week, you'd sit across the desk from a stranger and get pummeled with questions, one after another after another. I hated it. The social worker's office was not a place where I wanted to talk about anything. I just wanted to get outdoors and play.

Whenever I felt pushed by people—whether they were adults or kids—I pushed back. During therapy sessions, I'd start arguing matches that would serve no purpose, no function. Or else I would shut down, and practice spinning my basketball like the Harlem Globe Trotters, seeing if I could balance it on my finger until the clock said I could go. After all, I didn't know these people, and they didn't know me. For the most part, I just saw them as stupid. People looking to offer me help I didn't want or need.

I didn't talk about my past with the other kids at MacDonell's either, even my best friend Sarah. We were just trying to be normal, forget our hurts by refusing to face them. Somehow with Sister Janice, though, it was different. She'd pick me up at school after basketball practice or walk with me to my cottage before bed, and it felt easy to let her know about my life. We just talked—it wasn't some therapy session I was forced to sit through.

Most of all, Sister Janice made me feel like a normal kid. The one thing I resisted at all costs in those years was the label "orphan." Even after MacDonell's began to feel like home and the people around me became my new family, the shame over being abandoned was still palpable for me. I was sure I'd ended up in MacDonell's because I'd done something wrong, or just wasn't good enough. But try as I might, I couldn't figure out exactly where I'd faltered. Sister Janice helped me see past that. She helped me find redemption through her love.

Crossing the Bridge

the irises, thick textured vibrant purple splendor,
elegant in van gogh's gleam,
a slinking metallic pedaling tennis shoed line of gears,
handle bars and boys,
the blue black night swirling, deep broad chunky shimmers of
the starry night,
checkered smooth worn silver grating passing beneath the
knobby tires,
vivid vivacious faces celebrating, engaged, conversing, colors
popping off the canvas expressing life's fullness in Renoir's
mind's eye,
salty sheened smiles divinely innocent in unchecked laughter,
divine marble, chiseled, contoured, cultured, and cradled
proportions, elegant, David,
etched, grass cracked fingering sidewalks passing on pedals,
pillars of time, fallen, crumbled, the Parthenon,
keep up, stay in line, she's giggling, muted by the brown
straw hat,
majestic harmony, soothing notes, Moonlight Sonata, ears
peeled, simply Beethoven,
parked bikes, glass door clanking the pitted bell, anxious
exhalations,

trail of bubbles, black suited snorkels approached the busy reef,
one at a time, hurried, grinning, cone only, pink bubble gum,
chocolate, chocolate chip, rainbow sherbert, please,
life is bigger than here, life is larger than now, life is Your
greatest Dream,
regrouped, reseated, rounding the curves home, relishing each
one handed bite,
you can do anything you put your mind to,
pausing, picking, and parading quickly attained flowers for her
hat, doubled up laughter,
chase the fluffy white clouds, run the red poppy fields,
hold the golden sunflowers, praise the exquisite purple irises,
a small ride, a grand journey, an exquisite dance,
cross over your fears,
cross over…
the bridge.

Chapter 3

Karen

Moving into Laskey signaled a turning point. Before, with the younger boys in Hooper, there had been some rough moments when kids spun out of control, but generally we listened to our counselors and followed their lead. We saw them as allies, not enemies. Laskey was different. For many of the boys, part of proving yourself was showing how bad you could be—and how quickly you could run off the next person they assigned to take care of you. Especially if they didn't live up to your expectations.

Life for the counselors wasn't an easy ride, though we might not have seen it that way. They did everything for us: cooked us breakfast and fixed our snacks, made sure we took a bath and had clean clothes to wear, cut loose with us after school and watched TV or played board games with us at night. Essentially they were our parents, and like parents, they were with us 24/7; in my first years at MacDonell's, counselors worked seven days on, seven days off. Each cottage had a suite off the dining room where the counselor lived during his or her weeklong shift. So we got to know them real well. And it was pretty easy to tell who was going to stick around and who was going to leave.

A sure warning sign of a short-termer was someone who didn't know how to handle the kids' overall B.S. If they gave you a pass when you broke the rules, tried to buddy up to you, or acted like you were their equal, it was only a matter of time before they were out. Then there were the counselors who went rogue, didn't follow the orphanage structure, and thought they could handle things their own way. I would sit by watching them and think, "Ah, this is not cool." In fact, if I had a problem with how they managed us kids, I'd usually end up talking to Sister Janice about it.

Because MacDonell's was home for me for so long, I developed a real gift for picking out the short-termers and those who were in it for the long haul. And once I'd determined where a counselor stood, I'd make a decision about how much effort I was going to put into developing a relationship with her. From the outside, we may have looked like a rag-tag group of kids of every age and background. But in reality, we were one big family unit, and if you couldn't be what we needed you to be—a responsible, structured, caring adult—then you really didn't belong there.

* * *

By the time Karen showed up, the boys at Laskey had tested and scared off a few counselors, and were paying the price.

Punishment was being confined to campus: no field trips, no weekend ice-cream runs to the Scarlet Scoop, no bike rides down to the bayou. The Laskey boys hadn't been off the property, except to go to school, for two months. They were bad and they liked being bad. The game plan was to keep the momentum going. As someone new to this social structure—and also at the bottom of the totem pole—I decided to go along.

Little did we know that Karen had a plan of her own. She was going to win us over, come hell or high water. Not knowing what we were dealing with, the Laskey boys started things off with a bang.

Every morning, the cottage counselor was in charge of fixing us a hot meal before we went off to school, Saturday activities, or church. Dinner you ate in the dining hall, but breakfast was part of the morning routine in the cottage, along with making your bed, doing the dishes, and getting all your stuff together before you headed off for the bus. We had two long tables in the main room where all of us could sit—twelve boys and the counselor, who sat at the head of one table.

Karen decided to set the tone her first day by making us a really good breakfast. Good meal or not, we were ready for our newest challenge.

One of the house rules was wearing a shirt to the table. Drunk with the power of our previous exploits, most of the boys showed up bare-chested. But instead of giving in to the reaction we wanted, Karen ignored our mostly scrawny torsos, calmly served up our food, and sat down. Eyes met over the table. We needed to take it up a notch.

Soon we were hunched over our plates, eating. Suddenly, one of the boys snarled, "This food tastes like shit." "Oh, really?" Karen replied sweetly. "It tastes delicious to me." Before you knew it, a dozen voices joined in, griping and complaining about her carefully prepared meal. Karen looked around, unperturbed. "Listen," she said as she stood up. "I just want you all to just really enjoy it."

And with that she walked into her room and gently closed the door.

I don't know who threw the first biscuit, but within seconds, it was like a southern hailstorm of biscuits and silverware. I watched, hands at my sides, waiting for her bedroom door to fly open. Years later, Karen told me what she'd been doing on the other side of the wall that day. She stood there calmly, thinking just one thing:

"Sorry, boys, you all just don't know yet."

* * *

That night we had a meeting. Like Hooper, Laskey had a main room divided by a large bookcase down the center. The dining area was on one side, and a reading/TV room was on the other. The counselor's suite opened onto the dining room half. We sat on beanbag chairs in front of the TV to talk.

Albert, the most intimidating of the older boys, started it off. "Miss Jones lasted only two weeks. Then we ran Miss Ameker out of here. Now we have Miss Hardamo."(Although Karen's last name was Hardeman, Albert never could get his mouth around it—he'd been pretty neglected as a child, and his English was never very good.)

"That Miss Hardamo could take us two months," Albert continued.

We didn't know it, but while we were talking Karen had slipped out of her room and was standing on the other side of the divider, listening to us with a big old smile on her face.

That's when she decided that the way to win us over was to work a deal to get us off campus. That one act would put momentum on her side. Championship wrestling was the ticket.

* * *

Every month or two, East Park Recreation Center would hold a championship wrestling match with guys battling it out in the ring for a few bucks—it was early WWF, and pretty cheesy, but we were dying to go. We'd heard that Junk Yard Dog would be fighting in a few weeks, and we knew we had to be there.

Karen latched onto our juvenile desires and started working the wrestling angle. Soon she had us making our beds, doing the dishes, getting our homework done on time. All of our chores were on a point system, and you were rewarded with an allowance if you made all your points. We needed both the points and the money to get to championship wrestling night.

It probably wasn't the best event for a bunch of potential delinquents, but Karen knew that the means was going to justify the end. Five of us managed to make the cut, including Albert. A bunch more put their hearts into trying.

That Friday, Karen loaded the six of us into one of Mac-Donell's vans and we headed off for the match. The ring was set up in the recreation center's gym, with fold-out chairs all around. Karen respected our dignity by sitting one row back. Albert, Z, James, Robert, Clark, and I raged along with the crowd, screaming at the wrestlers and shooting them the occasional bird. Karen sat behind us, watching with amusement and shock that these little bitty boys had managed to intimidate so many people.

Her plan to win us over had worked.

* * *

The thing I loved about Karen was that she saw us not only for who we were but also for who we could be. She would put our complicated feelings about being orphans into perspective by saying, "Remember, this is just one small part of your life." That was something Karen had in common with Sister Janice: the ability to see a broken person presenting all the manifestations of their brokenness and yet know there was something unique and special underneath.

She noticed right away that I was a good, smart kid who had been served the injustice of landing in a family that didn't appreciate or want me. But she also noticed the one thing I tried to hide: I hated being touched.

After the wrestling match and in the weeks leading up to it, the atmosphere in the cottage had started to change, and the boys began to let Karen in. Slowly, she began re-implementing the rules: no bad language, no sneaking out at night, bedtime at ten, baths every day. As time went on, the guys would sit next to her on the long bench at the dining room table, hanging off of her like a bunch of monkeys. They respected her, but they also genuinely liked her. They'd be fooling with her hair, tugging at her sleeve, looking for attention. Sure, some of them were still playing hardcore, but you could see she'd definitely made some headway into our lives. I knew she and I had started to connect—but I would never have dreamed of grabbing her arm or putting my hand on her shoulder. I just didn't do that.

Silently, she began working on me, with a goal of making me feel comfortable with appropriate, friendly human touch. Counselors were not supposed to hug or kiss you—that was an unspoken rule—but she could sense that something inside me made me flinch even when our arms would accidently graze during dinner.

Little by little we got on a certain wavelength, and I began to let my guard down. Karen would ask me to fold laundry with her, occasionally letting our hands touch as we folded sheets or towels together. She also began working on my sense of self by bringing me skydiving or scuba diving magazines, and helping me dream about a life beyond MacDonell's.

But even though we talked a lot about the world outside Houma, she made sure I saw my surroundings clearly. And I did. I knew I was safe at the orphanage, that it was a good place, and that the people there really cared about me. Karen's goal was to prove through her actions that not everyone over twenty-five was a flaming alcoholic idiot—something most of the kids had seen way too much of. Instead she showed us what a sound, secure, kind adult looked like—someone who would be there for us, make life fun, and give us a window to a better future.

Brine in the Breeze

brine in the breeze,
the sweet crescent glow,
wispy grey fingers of moss,
the pitted face of lost shadows,
black water freckled by winged hunger,
passing luminate pillows,
worn elbows of creaking majesty,
twinkling yellow diamonds,
cracked fingers of fallen hands,
the black of eyes still as eternity,
my paused pace partially obscure,
the feathery dance partners of Night and Light,
embrace and release in forgotten passion,
i stand meeting ebony echoes,
gifts from the essence of birth,
i kneel to embrace the great Mother,
taste the sea,
caress the fine fingers,
listen to whispering grace,
she is beautiful,
she is divine,
she is angelic,
she is the pink dawn,
she is the purple set,
she is…

Chapter 4

Miss Armageddon

Once we had worked ourselves out of the hole we'd dug, the older boys at Laskey started to join in the regular activities off campus. There was always something going on—camping on the beach, picking pecans, going to Grand Isle, or just riding your bike downtown on a Saturday afternoon. One of my favorites was fishing and crabbing with Sister Ellen.

Sister Ellen came to MacDonell's shortly after Sister Janice took over as school administrator. They had worked together at another orphanage in Marrero, on the west bank in New Orleans, before coming to MacDonell's. Unlike our home, Hope Haven-Madonna Manor was a Catholic charity, and it was run by the School Sisters of Notre Dame, the order Janice and Ellen belonged to. Sister Ellen had been the principal at the school that was part of the boys' orphanage.

About the time Sister Janice took the administrative position in Houma, the order sent Sister Ellen back to school to get her master's degree, and in the summertime she joined us at Mac-Donell's to help out with recreation. Ellen was a native Louisianan who had grown up in a big family out in the country, and she knew how to do all kinds of stuff we liked to do: mechanics, woodworking, making stained glass, fixing up bikes. But there was nothing she loved more than going fishing on the bayou.

Summer days, when we'd be out of school, we'd head down to Port Fourchon or some other place on the Gulf and spend the day catching speckled trout and redfish or crabs. To crab, you'd tie raw chicken onto string, cast it out, and when the string started to tug, gently pull in your crab and net him. By late afternoon, our coolers would be full of live shellfish crawling all over each other trying to escape.

Back at MacDonell's that night, Mrs. Joseph or one of the other ladies from the kitchen would have big pots of water boiling on the stove, ready to go. They'd drop in our squirming catch, fixing up a crab boil with red potatoes, corn, sausage, and Cajun spices. It was a lot of work, but man did we have fun. Sitting at dinner that night, I'd look around and see happy kids plowing through crab dripping with butter, lemon juice, and hot sauce. My friend Sarah, who'd spent the first years of her life hungry and neglected, would catch my eye and smile. No matter what direction life ended up taking any of us, those days were good memories we could hold onto forever.

* * *

Sister Ellen joined MacDonell's full-time once she finished up her master's in Thibodaux a year and a half later. Sister Janice put her in charge of recreation and education—the perfect fit for her feisty personality.

I say feisty because as much as Sister Ellen loved to have a good time, there was never a question of who was in charge. You'd see her walking around with her clipboard on campus or spot her at school, heading over to talk with the principal about one or another of us MacDonell's kids, and you knew you'd better do what she expected of you, even if it wasn't your first choice. In some ways, she was the bad cop to Sister Janice's good cop. She'd go over your homework in study hall, and if it looked like you were trying to pass one over on her, she'd actually reread the chapter herself and say, "Did you even read this? Read it again. Rewrite your questions. You can do better." In our eyes, it felt like she was our own personal Miss Armageddon.

But the thing was, she always had a great sense of humor under that drill sergeant exterior. She could defuse even the most antagonistic situations, getting you to laugh just when you thought things were about to blow up. No matter what you felt about having to do your homework, you couldn't help but like Sister Ellen.

Being in charge of recreation served as the perfect foil to managing our academic lives. MacDonell's already had an intensive rec program when Sister Ellen arrived, but she made it even bigger and better. In addition to fishing trips and swimming lessons, we did all kinds of arts and crafts—ceramics, macramé, stained glass, painting, carpentry. It was fun to make stuff and show off your creativity. But there was more to it than that. Some of things we made filled an even greater need.

When you live with thirty-five other kids, even when all your physical requirements are being taken care of, something is missing. No matter how well you're being fed, what clothes you wear, or how warm your bed is, you still need a sense of privacy and some personal space. Being the second child in a family of fifteen kids, Sister Ellen understood that. And so she started us building padlocked boxes for our private stuff.

It took a lot of thought. First we'd choose the wood we wanted to use and prep it, depending on if we planned to paint or stain it. Then we'd determine how big we wanted the box to be, what design we wanted it to have, whether we'd add stickers or other decorations. It might seem like a small thing, but it felt significant. Living in a cottage with twelve other adolescent boys, there wasn't much you could call your very own.

Whether it was making a strong meter joint or firing a pot correctly in ceramics or getting a good grade on a test at school, Sister Ellen also taught us the value of doing our best work. She and Sister Janice just straight out expected it. If you did a shoddy job and got mad when one of them pointed it out, they'd say, "Well, what do you want me to think, that you're stupid or crazy or incapable?" They were showing us that no matter what our circumstances, people should expect good things from us because we were perfectly capable of achieving them. It was when others stopped holding us to high standards that we should start worrying. They knew that if we took responsibility, our success would breed success.

* * *

Pretty early on, Sister Ellen tagged me as someone with skills who needed some room to prove himself. It wasn't long afterward that my bike repair job took off.

Every year, the home would get bikes from the Houma Police Department that had been stolen and never claimed. Most of them were in pretty bad shape—broken chains, chipped paint, flat tires, or shot brake pads. Sister Ellen was good at fixing them. She could strip off the paint, replace the bearings, fix the broken parts, and put them all back together—then each kid at MacDonell's would have their own bike to ride around, pretty much free of charge to the home.

But just because she could do it didn't mean she felt she should. Sister Ellen saw right away that the bikes were an opportunity to teach kids self-reliance.

So she showed me how to do a bicycle. I learned how to disassemble the parts, burn off the paint, fix a derailleur or an out-of-whack caliper, and replace an inner tube. Before long, I could handle the whole process on my own, and pretty soon, as demand for rehabbed bikes increased, I taught Bobby B. to do it, then Robert S. Now all of a sudden we had a network of three guys who had this valuable skill—and people around campus looked up to us for it. I liked being the go-to guy. It helped me overcome a lot of my own self-doubt and self-fear.

* * *

It took me a little longer to feel good about how things were going at school. I continued concentrating more on goofing around and sports, and was managing to bring home average grades, until the day I made a D in English on my report card.

Sisters Ellen and Janice saw that as a major red flag, and all of a sudden I inherited two study halls a day. I had to bring home my books from every class subject Monday through Friday, and Sister Ellen and I would review all five or six courses. That experience forced me to learn good study skills and how to manage my time better—things that would come in very handy once I left MacDonell's later in life.

But it wasn't an easy lesson. I'd much rather have been shooting hoops with my friends or joining the team on the field for batting practice. What Sister Ellen told me was this: "There are specific rules that society mandates that you have to follow. You have to learn how to live within the structures society presents. You don't have to accept them, but to be a productive young man or woman when you leave this place, you have to know how to follow the rules or how to disagree with them logically." It was her way of telling me she loved me and wanted me to succeed, and behaving well in school and getting good grades were the keys to my success.

"Love" wasn't a word you heard much at MacDonell's. Everyone on staff was very careful not to use it, because love had such a twisted meaning for so many of the kids. Instead Sister Janice and Sister Ellen would say, "You know I care about you." And we did. They were there for us 24/7, their families were at a distance, and they had put their personal lives on hold. Unlike in our biological homes, at MacDonell's love didn't include being physically, psychologically, or verbally abused. There were boundaries, and we needed those boundaries, sometimes desperately. But we also needed the expectations that come with love, and that's where the sisters came in. Our family at MacDonell's, headed up by nuns and including children of every race and background, required us to be responsible for our own lives.

Miss Armageddon

Board Games

We would all watch one by one their excited departures
We would all watch, aware we were not leaving
We would all watch till we had to slip off in lonely silence
We would all know we were there for the stark leftovers
We would all take in the turkey from the night before
We would all stay in the same cottage
We would all go to sleep in loneliness
We would all wake up and know it was just another holiday
spent with our discarded family
We would all find comfort together playing Board Games
We would all in our own way give thanks for each other
We would all.

CHAPTER 5

Christmas at Home

Sister Ellen kept us busy with arts and crafts projects year-round, but at Christmastime she amped things up a notch. She liked to say, "It's important to give, not only to get," and during the holidays, she made sure we all embraced the giving spirit.

The first order of business after everyone returned from their Thanksgiving family visits was the Christmas gift drawing. Sister Ellen would gather us together after dinner one night in late November, and each child would draw a name from a big bowl. It was never an option not to participate, or to say that you didn't like the person you had picked. That slip of paper represented your secret Christmas friend, and it was binding.

Throughout the first weeks in December, the arts and crafts room was filled with eight or ten kids every afternoon after school and on the weekends too. We put our all into being as creative as possible. Though you weren't supposed to tell anyone who you were making your gift for, part of the fun was guessing who was making what for whom. Anyone could be a match, and sometimes the best gifts came out of the most unlikely pairs: elementary school kids and high schoolers, withdrawn children and bullies, short-term placements who would soon be released to foster care and long-timers like me.

I always felt the gift exchange brought everyone closer together, made us kinder and more caring toward one another. I know that for most of us, it was the first time we'd experienced what it was like to have a healthy and loving place to celebrate the holidays.

* * *

The days quickly rolled by, and soon it was the week before Christmas. We always had our big Christmas dinner the Thursday before school let out, a much-anticipated night to remember.

Mrs. Crochet, wearing her long white apron and just a touch of makeup for the holidays, would direct the older kids as they covered the dining room tables in pressed white linen and decorated them with fresh holly wreaths. Each wreath encircled a well-polished silver candle holder holding a tall white taper. On that night and for our Thanksgiving celebration, the ornate fine china would be brought out and polished to a high gleam. Only a few of the older boys and girls had the honor of serving and clearing during holiday dinners, since they were less likely to drop or break the china.

The year I was finally chosen to be a server, I went early to the dining room wearing my normal school clothes. Living at MacDonell's, I had learned how to set a table, to serve from the left and retrieve from the right, and arrange silverware from the outside in, in the order it would be used. After setting up, I rushed back to my cottage to change into my Sunday best along with the other kids before we all returned for the big celebration.

By the time we got back, the candles had been lit and their flickering glow whispered to everyone still enough to listen. The old hardwood floors, meticulously cleaned and polished, reflected the glow with their own muted shine. It took a few moments to get everyone to their assigned seats and quiet them for the evening prayer. The overhead lights dimmed, Sister Janice chose one of the younger kids to say grace, and the servers silently stood and filed into the kitchen, returning with plates of turkey and ham, yams and dressing, green beans, fresh bread, and pecan pie made from the pecans we had picked ourselves.

The whole evening had a transformational effect. It forced us to reach beyond our inner lives and focus on one another—and to experience the giving spirit of Christmas as every child, no matter what their circumstances, should.

* * *

Besides bringing excitement and joy, however, the holiday season also brought the realization that soon I would be left behind at MacDonell's with the handful of kids who never went home. Watching the others go one by one filled me with emptiness and an overwhelming feeling of hurt.

The staff noticed and did all they could to ease us through those quiet weeks. On Christmas morning, they showered me, Tina, Clark, and James—the four lone refugees—with gifts. They let us all move into one of the cottages so we could be together at night and stay up late playing board games. Certain staff members made a point of working through the holidays, or they'd stop by after spending Christmas with their own families to give us some extra attention. Karen was there, every December. She'd do everything she could think of to show us a good time—take us to the movies, over to her mother's house, down to the roller rink for an afternoon of skating. She was simply there for us. Even that terrible Christmas Dad and my stepmother Dale finally decided to let us come home.

* * *

For years, I had listened to the boys in my cottage and the other kids around campus brag on how great their daddies were, how their mommas missed them and that soon they'd be going home for good. Watching how things went after they returned from weekends at home or holidays with their folks, I knew it was bull. They'd come back to MacDonell's after a few days with their messed-up parents and you could just see the sullenness oozing out of their pores. Some of the more violent kids, like Albert, would be like walking tornadoes, angry and out of control. Others, like Sarah and her sister Hilda, would look shell-shocked or dismayed by what they'd experienced. But most put up a front anyway, and you really couldn't blame them for that.

I had my hopes too. My stepbrother's wife, Patty, had somehow figured out that Dad had three kids he'd abandoned at the local orphanage, and she just couldn't get her mind around it. "Wait a minute, these are your kids and you don't even visit them?" she railed at him when she found out. Pretty soon she became our cheerleader, and Dad and Dale, probably just wanting to shut her up, finally agreed to bring us home for Christmas.

I had to admit, I was kind of excited. I hadn't seen my family for years, and finally Tina and I could be like the other kids, pack a suitcase and actually have someone show up to take us home. Plus, I knew Patty was level-headed and had some intelligence. It would be cool to hang out with her and get to know her better.

But then we got there, and reality set in. There were Dad and Dale, Drunk and Drunk, tolerating having us home just so they could use and abuse us.

It was chaos, one long party fueled by alcohol and fighting, and Tina and I became Dad and Dale's slaves, there literally to clean up the mess. All I kept thinking was, "This is it? This is my family? This is what I've got?" Looking around, it became crystal clear that I was not their class of person. These were mean and hurtful people, their house stank and they were constantly yelling. Why had I ever thought things would be different?

Dale had always been violent toward me—maybe because I wasn't afraid to fight back or maybe because I looked different from all the other kids, and from my dad. The rest of the Burases were stocky and dark, but I was lean and fair. And although it was clear that Dale didn't want any of us in her life, not even sweet little Tina, with me the animosity went deeper. It was like she hated me before she even knew me, that I was a target she needed to punish every single day.

One night, in a fit of drunkenness, Dale went off the deep end. On the table next to the couch they had a shellacked piece of coral mounted on a base that someone had picked up at a resort on the Gulf. This thing was heavy and sharp—it probably weighed three or four pounds. As she was screaming at me for the millionth time, Dale grabbed the coral and chucked it at my head, hard. I had just enough time to turn my face away before the massive weight hit me square on. In seconds, the side of my head was throbbing with pain, and I could feel warm, thick blood pouring from my ear and temple down the side of my face. Fortunately, Patty was there. She grabbed me, pulled me out of the trailer with Tina, and hurried us down the street to the trailer where she lived with my stepbrother. That night, Tina and I stayed on her couch. Patty drove us back to MacDonell's the following day, making sure the abrasions to my ear had stopped bleeding sufficiently.

By the time we arrived at the orphanage, I was past being scared or hurt. Fury filled every cell of my body. I stomped up the sidewalk toward Laskey, then looked up to see Karen, quietly watching from the doorway. She held the door open and I marched past her, through the shared living space and down the hallway to my room.

Karen found me an hour later sitting on my bed, arms crossed over my chest and my face turned to the wall. She had just one thing to say: "It sure is a shame you're going to be sick tomorrow and have to stay home from school." I looked up gratefully. I knew she was offering me a gift. We could talk about it then, watch a little *Price Is Right,* and have some peace and quiet before the rest of the kids got home.

Though they weren't connected to me by blood, God had blessed me with a family who loved me and whom I could truly call my own.

Oh, Sister

Hold my shaking hand,
Walk with me this crooked mile,
Gathering endless pecans,
Playful blue water swimming,
Dreaming beneath the outstretched arms of Live Oaks,
Blue lipped bubble gum snow cones,
Rib splitting laughter till rolling joyful tears,
Running below stars, hide-n-seek, giggles everywhere,
Miles of meandered biking, exploring, wide eyed amazement,
Screaming, breathless, white knuckled roller coasters,
Making, creating, giving Christmas Gifts,
Working for a greater awareness,
Courage to walk through Our Fears,
Giving Unconsciously,
Sharing Unconditionally,
My family,
My Sister,,,,,,

Always,
Your Brother

CHAPTER 6

Sister Sarah

Part of my family was a girl my age that I came to think of as my sister.

I met Sarah the very first day I came to MacDonell's. She lived in Keener, and Tina was matched up to be her roommate. Because of that, I made a point of watching Sarah closely to make sure she would take care of my tiny, timid little sister. She was just the right person to ease Tina into our new home.

Sarah had already lived at the children's home for more than two years when we arrived. Like me, she came with a sibling: her sister Hilda. Sarah's older brother Joe had been placed there ahead of them, but they were too young to join him at the time. Normally, MacDonell's didn't accept kids under the age of six because they weren't old enough to go to school. But Sarah's family situation was bad, so as soon as she turned six, Mac-Donell's found a place for her—and for Hilda, who was only four. Sister Janice and Sister Ellen knew that part of these girls' survival was staying together. When either Sarah or Hilda talked about "me," they were always speaking for both of them.

Sarah and I connected right away; she was just easy to be around. From the outside we seemed very different, me somewhat sarcastic and precocious with a quick wit and temper, Sarah quiet and shy, compliant and pretty guarded. But I could see in the way she protected Tina that we had a lot in common too. I could trust Sarah, she was kind to the other kids, and she was smart.

Both of us, and our siblings, were there for the long haul, so we had lots of time to get to know each other. Like the Buras kids, Sarah and Hilda never went home to their natural families on the weekends or for holidays. Various family members or foster parents would pick them up, and from the look on the girls' faces when they came home, it didn't seem like a good situation. Sarah and I also tended to be in the same place at the same time, on campus or at school. Because we were almost exactly the same age—just one day apart—we were in the same classes, had the same study halls, and participated in the same activities at the home, which were arranged according to your age. Even though Sarah was average athletically, she was always willing to play whatever game the kids at MacDonell's got started on our makeshift athletic field: softball, volleyball, basketball, tag. Pretty soon, we started choosing one another when it came time to pick teams.

For some great reason, Sarah just got me, and I got her. Other kids on campus could be timid around me because I had a temper and wasn't afraid to let it show, but not Sarah. We were totally comfortable hanging out together. That could be hard to find at the children's home because of all the damage kids carried around with them, mental scars and bruises that they revealed with aggression, mind games, and other nasty behavior. It wasn't just the Laskey boys who could mix things up; the girls had their own way of getting what they wanted out of weak kids or counselors.

Because she was quiet, Sarah might have looked weak too, but she had her own way of managing the bullies. She was really good at blending in. There was a hierarchy among all the kids, girls and boys, based on age, dominance, popularity, and talent—basically a page torn out from a middle-school playbook. Kids tended to follow the loudmouth rather than the thinker, and you were always hoping the playing field would balance out with kids who played fair. Sarah was someone who did.

Even though we got to be best friends over time, Sarah and I rarely spoke about our biological families or why we'd ended up in a children's home. Like all the kids at MacDonell's, we were just trying to make it, trying to be normal and fit in. To do that, we left our hurts unspoken. But little by little, by watching and gathering clues over the years, I figured out what had happened to Sarah.

Some of it she told me outright: she came from a very poor family with six kids, her dad was a lot older than her mom and he worked hard to make ends meet, and they'd lived in an abandoned school bus, with no plumbing or electricity. Other stuff Sarah didn't say outright, but I saw the signs: her mother had been abusive and neglectful and both parents were easy prey for those around them, making survival even harder. As a result, at a young age Sarah and Hilda were taken from their family and placed in series of foster homes, sometimes with relatives, sometimes with strangers. In nearly all of them, the girls were barely existing, sleeping on the floor or sharing a bed with several other people, not getting enough to eat, and experiencing the same kind of negative or violent attention from their foster parents that I'd experienced from Simon and Dale.

She had been lucky in one respect. A young minister befriended her father and took Sarah and Hilda under his wing.

He ended up serving in the role of social worker, first to get them out of the school bus and into foster homes, and eventually to get the girls into MacDonell's. For a short while before they came to the orphanage, Sarah and Hilda had even lived with him, and those were happy memories.

Coming to MacDonell's felt even more hopeful than living with the minister. For the first time, Sarah had a bed of her own, a closet and things to put in it, good food, warm baths, gifts on birthdays and holidays, trips and vacations, and regular school and church. Like me, she embraced the structure and stability. MacDonell's was different for us from our biological homes because it was a place where our thoughts mattered, and as long as we were respectful, our voices counted.

Pretty soon Sarah and I became inseparable. We sat together in the crafts room, and I always saved her a seat in the van when we were going fishing or to the zoo. She felt comfortable enough around me to let her guard down. My goofy jokes and outgoing nature made her feel like she could tell me things she didn't share with other people: her dreams, her secrets, her fears. I felt the same way with her. Unlike with most people, I knew I could trust Sarah, and that she wouldn't judge me, even when I got frustrated and mad. We had mutual respect and understanding, which for kids dealing with constant change and transition was rare.

She was guarded with anyone new or unfamiliar, though, just like me. That included Sister Janice and Sister Ellen when they showed up not long after I did. Sarah had bonded with some of the staff who were there when she arrived: Mr. Cox, who ran the children's home before Sister Janice, Mrs. Crochet in the dining hall, and Miss Stone, who was a counselor at Keener. Like anybody would, she'd gotten used to the way things were run, and she was suspicious of change.

Because they'd worked at a boys' orphanage before coming to MacDonell's, the sisters' initial focus was on masculine things: repairing bikes, going fishing, playing sports, building stuff. We Laskey boys loved it, but the girls complained, including Sarah. It was a learning curve for everyone. Then pretty soon Sister Ellen added ceramics classes, gardening, painting, and sewing, and things started to even out. Everything revolved around teaching us how to do things for ourselves, be responsible, and show our talents and ability to learn new things. We might not have admitted it, but even the boys liked the arts and crafts, especially at Christmastime, and I treasured the pillow Sarah made me that spelled out "Paul" the year she drew my name in the annual gift exchange.

I don't remember when we first started thinking about each other as brother and sister rather than just friends. It just sort of naturally happened. We even fought like brother and sister, nagged and teased each other on the bus or while we did homework together. Janice and Ellen encouraged the friendship we shared, knowing that in our own way, we were forming a family we could rely on. Long after we left MacDonell's, the sisters made sure Sarah and I continued to stay in touch. "Have you heard from your sister Sarah?" "Have you written back to your brother?" they'd ask us. When either Sarah or I visited Janice and Ellen, we'd get on the phone so the four of us could talk as a family.

Somehow, even in our adolescent years, our friendship never turned to romance. It would have been like kissing Tina to kiss my sister Sarah. And besides, anything involving touch was off limits for both of us. But we always knew how we felt about one another, even if we didn't say it or show it physically.

When you've been tossed around like Sarah and I had been, it can be hard to know how people really feel about you. You know how you feel, but you're never really sure about the other person. With Sarah, I was sure. We were siblings for life.

Sister Sarah

The Pit

Eager elbows,
Spirited pursuit,
Intrepid vision,
Gnawing ambition,
Hungered eyes,
Unwavered task,
Palms of callous,
Active awareness,
Vigorous thighs,
Blind ambition,
Courageous lungs,
Zealous plans,
Clawing resourcefulness,
Endeavored optimist,
Deft balance,
Black eyed,
Long on tail,
My stench, My rot,
My pit, My prize, My kingdom,
Ooooops . . . dash down the hole!!

CHAPTER 7

The Entrepreneur

It was early evening and I was hustling across the bumpy oyster-shell-lined parking lot pushing my rickety, rusty red wheelbarrow, trying to keep it steady at my hurried pace. Finally I reached my destination, and I hadn't tipped my heavy load. It was the first day of my new voluntary job: Mr. B's garbage assignment.

Mr. Bridges was the orphanage director, someone who stayed mostly in the background at MacDonell's, so getting an assignment from him was a pretty big deal, and I was prepared to do my best work.

I slung open the doors to the garbage pit as hard as I could. Instantly, I was blinded. A huge swarm of flapping brown wings filled the air, obscuring my vision. Aaaaah! In terror and disgust I fell backward into the bed of my wheelbarrow, slapping at the massive flying cockroaches. I couldn't pull myself from the unsteady metal cart so I frantically swatted off the hard-shelled bodies still crawling on me. My arms backpedaled and I struggled to keep from yelling in order to prevent any bugs from getting in my mouth. Finally, the last cockroach flew off into the pale dusk. I gasped, catching my breath. The encounter had felt biblical. But by the end of the week, my pocket would be $1.50

richer. For that price, I was willing to handle a little plague and pestilence.

* * *

At MacDonell's, each of the children got a weekly allowance, but you had to earn it. The payout varied, depending on how well you did your daily chores, how clean you kept your room, and your behavior day by day. Best case scenario, you got $1.50 a week; worst case, fifty cents. Since candy bars cost a quarter and a trip to the movies was a buck, it was actually a pretty good deal.

The point system went like this: you were graded from zero (the worst) to five (perfection) on each of the three components of your score every day. From there, it got more complicated. Get a zero, one, or two for your daily work and behavior, and you lost—or at least didn't gain—overall points. You had to get at least a four to maintain a positive cumulative score. The numbers were tallied at the end of the week, your allowance was calculated from the sum, and you either suffered the consequences of bad work and behavior or reaped the rewards of doing well.

Being creative, adaptable, and persistent, I made it my goal to make as much money as possible from the system—and more, if I could find extra paying jobs to supplement my allowance.

Keeping my room neat was easy. I always scored high marks for making my bed and keeping my closet and chest of drawers tidy. My room later became a showcase for the younger kids to model. Chores included things like washing and drying breakfast and snack dishes, sweeping the main rooms of the cottage, and clearing the table after meals. Behavior grading was more subjective, and being the clown I was, I had to work harder to score fives with my counselors. It took a while to figure out what was expected of you to make a perfect five.

One place where negative behavior could knock down your score was in the dining hall. Each week, the four cottages at MacDonell's—Hooper, Laskey, Keener, and Downs—rotated dinner clean-up duty. Mrs. Crochet, the cook and organizer who had grown up at MacDonell's herself, patiently orchestrated us. We set tables and cleared plates, scraped dishes coming out of the dining room after dinner, washed, dried, and put everything away. You could only be dismissed to go to study hall when everything was spotless. There weren't any points rewarded for doing dining hall work, but you could be dinged up to three points if you had a bad attitude. Mrs. Crochet would watch us closely, and if you goofed off or did sloppy work, she'd have to call your cottage and report the bad behavior to your counselor.

Not cleaning your plate at the table could also get you a bad score. That usually wasn't a problem for me, except in the infamous case of the bread pudding.

After-school snacks were a regular part of our day, and most of the staff knew our favorites. Homemade brownies, cupcakes, and cookies always put a smile on your face after a long day at school. But one of the counselors, Mrs. B, decided that bread pudding was the world's best afternoon snack, sometimes serving it three times a week even while she watched us suffer through bowl after bowl. It was horrible—lumpy, clumpy, and dense as a rock. But you had to eat every bite or suffer the penalty of a negative behavior mark.

Since there wasn't a family dog lying under the table to secretly feed spoonfuls to, napkins soon became my own personal bread pudding graveyard. I'd take a little bite, tuck a big spoonful in the napkin, repeat. That well-worn trick saved me many hours of sitting at the table, staring down a bowl of lead.

* * *

You could also make extra money at MacDonell's by doing volunteer chores. One of my earliest paying jobs—only given to the responsible younger boys—was putting up the flag each morning after breakfast and taking it down before dark. It earned me an extra fifty cents a week. But more than that, raising the flag taught me about daily commitment. Only really bad rain mixed with lightning could get you out of flag duty. Each morning another boy and I would respectfully unfurl the stars and stripes, then, when it came time to put the flag away, precisely fold the large banner, never letting it touch the ground.

Other small jobs that earned me extra points and pennies were folding clothes, matching socks, and the weekly Wednesday garbage duty. To earn the big bucks, I knew I'd have to swallow my hatred of grime and bad smells, going beyond Mr. B's garbage assignment to take on cleanup of the garbage pit.

A four-by-eight-foot slab of dark gray, cracked concrete was the center for garbage disposal. Various-sized green and gray garbage cans, packed side-by-side three rows deep and nine wide, tottered on the uneven slab. The garbage from all four cottages ended up here, as well as the nightly scraps and trash from the dining hall. The smell was rancid, rotten enough to make your toes curl, but for three dollars a week I'd learn to tough it through.

All the kids hated to take out the trash, so the pit was a mess. Garbage was strewn all over the place. I'd make a daily after-school visit to the pit to keep things tidy before the Saturday garbage truck run, then hose the whole thing down on the weekend.

The pit was also home to a pack of aggressive, large rats and the occasional hissing possum. They couldn't stay away from the never-ending food source, no matter how many times we chased them off with rocks. There were a bunch of holes in the wire stretched to enclose the pit, and rats would appear and disappear in an instant, or jump out of one of the cans as you tossed stuff in, landing on your feet. They terrified the little kids. It was easy to see why children would fling the garbage in the general direction of a trash bin then run for their lives, dragging that rusty wheelbarrow behind them.

The garbage pit job was neverending, come rain or come shine. But I was just as determined to maximize my earning potential.

* * *

Pretty soon, I was coming up with schemes of my own to make money. Back behind the dining hall, Sister Ellen and Mrs. Crochet had Mr. Crochet till up a plot to make a garden, and each boy and girl was offered a row. Most took half; I took three. Soon my corn, green bean, tomato, and watermelon seeds were in the ground, and I added weeding to my list of things to do before bedtime each night. The corn sprouted up quickly and looked promising, but my work was foiled by some nasty brown worms that made themselves at home inside the bright green husks. The darn birds ate up all my tomatoes, and the watermelon never developed past the size of a softball. But those beans grew and grew, and along with them, my visions of wealth.

Harvest time came, and first I approached Mrs. Crochet, pitching fresh produce for a price. She smiled and held back full-on laughter, then graciously declined. I regained my composure and headed off to the cottages. Surely the counselors would want to buy fresh produce to take home to their own kitchens? "No" was the consistent reply.

So I hauled my beans back to Mrs. Crochet and grudgingly donated them to the home.

My next entrepreneurial scheme was taking and selling pictures. I'd bought a Kodak 110 with some of my savings and took it everywhere—field trips, outings, around campus. One day while snapping shots of a tag football game, I had a Eureka moment—I'd take pictures of the other kids and sell them back to the orphanage! They could use them for marketing, to share with the board of directors and our sponsors, even print my photos on the home's official letterhead. Mr. B liked my idea. Then he politely said no.

* * *

Despite my failures, people noticed my hard work and energy. Sister Ellen and Sister Janice complimented my creativity and determination. Karen continued to encourage me to think beyond the confines of my young life to what lay ahead. And the other kids saw me as a leader—I'd been around so long and done so much.

By the time I got to high school, I'd been at MacDonell's for six years, longer than almost any other orphan there. I'd seen dozens of kids come and go. Some went back to their families, others were adopted out, and a few were sent to reform schools or other facilities. But I stayed on.

My longevity and attitude brought with them advantages beyond money. I was one of the few kids who earned trip passes to go visit my school friends at their houses in town. One Sunday afternoon, I even joined my Sunday school teacher and his family to go ice skating in Baton Rouge. Eventually I had an after-school job dipping ice cream at the Scarlet Scoop, which allowed me to finally save what I considered to be a lot of money at the time. I could actually afford a brand name T-shirt and blue jeans, which were always on my wish list.

No matter what my school or work commitments, I was always involved in sports and other activities too. Track was by far what I enjoyed most. I earned a place on the varsity team as the pole-vaulter—at first by default. I later went on to become the parish champ my senior year, and placed third in regionals.

I think the people around me, including the other kids, saw what I was capable of and set the bar higher for me. I'd toughed it out with the worst of them, boxing bullies until they finally viewed me as their equal and left me alone. When I encountered boys and girls of any age who couldn't defend themselves, I jumped in. I felt a deep sense of responsibility for protecting those who couldn't defend themselves, even though I never started a fight. Eventually, I realized the much more important role of leading by example and setting standards for better behavior among all the kids on the campus. There was definitely a learning curve to what drove my actions. When I was younger, I had the ability to persuade others in order to achieve my own selfish outcomes. Time and maturity taught me there was a better way to live and give back.

Through it all, I knew that there was something special about my place at the orphanage. I was part of a minority that was going to make it out of MacDonell's and achieve something significant with their lives. It gave me pride to recognize that. Looking around, I could see the kids who wouldn't be able to overcome the bad hand they'd been dealt. I could feel it, and it made me sad to know they were going to repeat the cycle their parents had set.

But that wasn't me. I was going to be someone.

The Entrepreneur

The Constancy of Acceptance

The humbling awareness of feeling I am loved,
The kneeling humility of tearful healing,
The Consciousness of Amazing Grace,
The Joyful tears accepting my lost and lonely boys,
The ache of spirit that feels, I have not done enough,
The consciousness of lost and lonely orphaned friends,
The lonely tears in loving spirit,
The clarity of accepting lost dreams.
The Constancy of Acceptance quietly, calmly,
and unconditionally brings a breath of healing
that transcends all that I know.

In Amazing Grace ,,,,

The Constancy of Acceptance thrives everlasting.

CHAPTER 8

Redemption

Sister Janice and Sister Ellen had the same hope for all the children at MacDonell's—that they would make it out of the orphanage with tools that would allow them to function well as adults, and eventually contribute to society. Some kids were easier to reach than others. The level of abuse and neglect that we had experienced before ending up at the orphanage left scars that could run very deep.

In some cases there were visible reminders of abuse. It wasn't unusual to notice marks on kids' arms and legs the size and shape of a cigarette tip. One boy had scar tissue on the palms of his hands where his mother had held them to the burners on the family stove. With other children, you couldn't see any physical traces of their pain. Instead, a memory from their past would trigger an outburst of rage. One child on campus had been tied to metal bedsprings for hours on end as his form of punishment at home. He would wake up in the night screaming, and Sister Janice would calm him and let him know, without ever putting it into words, that he was safe at MacDonell's in a way he had never been safe with his own parents.

The sense of calm, of order and normalcy the nuns gave us went a long way toward healing our pain. It was how they nurtured us instead of giving physical comfort, because anything physical had such a twisted meaning for us. For the same reason, Sister Ellen and Sister Janice didn't believe in corporal punishment. Most of MacDonell's children had seen plenty of that before they arrived. It was why boys like Albert Jones resorted to fist-fighting for even the smallest offense—no discussion, no questions asked. For him and lots of the others, the way you dealt with frustration was to lash out. It was a standard, automatic reaction, like breathing.

Sister Janice and Sister Ellen tried to show us a different way. If you had a problem with one of your counselors, for example, they'd talk to you and have you go back and deal with the counselor yourself, rationally. If the nuns had taken on the issue directly instead of having you resolve your own problems, the lesson would have been lost. Their method was so subtle we didn't even realize we were being taught new ways to relate to others. Their goal was that all those little actions would add up and eventually break the cycle of violence we all knew so well.

* * *

After leaving MacDonell's, I learned that Karen called Sister Janice "the original velvet brick." I loved that because it fit so well. Sister Janice gave us a foundation and a sense of permanence, but she did it softly, gently, with unwavering patience. It wasn't a technique we were used to, and it made everyone want to fall into her grace. There was no manipulation; she genuinely wanted you to become better, to improve your place in life, and to prop up your sense of self-worth and self-esteem. In the process she gave you the sense of belonging that you had always longed for, the feeling that you were finally, in some sense of the term, somebody's child.

Sister Janice's calling had always been to work with children living in orphanages. After I became an adult, she told me that from the time she was a teenager, she'd dreamt constantly about becoming a nun who would help abandoned and neglected kids. She'd graduated high school early, at age sixteen, then took her vows the next year, with her parents' permission. Her family consisted of seven children, but the two siblings before Janice had died during infancy. Her mother told Janice that when she was born, it was like a new life had come to help the family heal from its loss. That sense of love and of life being a gift served as a model for what Sister Janice later gave the children under her care.

The order both Janice and Ellen belonged to was the School Sisters of Notre Dame. It was founded to provide education to poor children and care for orphans. The community had run the Madonna Manor orphanage in New Orleans as part of its mission, and Sister Janice worked there for fourteen years, serving in the roles of teacher, housemother, director of recreation, and business manager before moving into administration. Then the Sisters of Notre Dame decided they no longer wanted to administer Madonna Manor, that they would merge it with its sister home, Hope Haven, eliminating her job. The merger was painful for Sister Janice to watch. It signaled a change in the direction of the community, from overseeing orphanages, whose numbers were dwindling, to focusing solely on education. Although MacDonell's was a Methodist home, Mr. Bridges hired Sister Janice as administrator after she left Madonna Manor, allowing her to continue to serve her calling and maintain ties to the community that would soon no longer serve the mission she had dedicated her life to.

* * *

Mr. B wasn't the only one who recognized that Sister Janice—and later, Sister Ellen—had a gift. Karen and others on staff saw it too. It was clear both nuns could have been successful in many things, and yet they devoted their lives to orphaned children.

Karen understood this because she was following the same path. Though she seemed old to me when she arrived, Karen was only in her early twenties. She'd had some wild years growing up, but had embraced Christ at twenty-one. I don't think Z or James or any of us really thought about what a sacrifice it was for a young, lively woman like Karen to come and live with twelve pre-teen and teenage boys. She was on duty for seven days at a time, and on her days off, she lived in a room she rented from an elderly lady in Houma. It wasn't the life most fun-loving twenty-three-year-olds would have dreamed of, but Karen saw it as a job she was meant to do, as her own spiritual calling.

Just like Sister Janice and Sister Ellen, Karen was also there to pick up the pieces when the rage from our past overwhelmed us. She got punched in the eye twice when she stepped in to calm down out-of-control boys, and even though they felt sorry when tempers cooled, it couldn't have been easy for her to walk around town with a big black eye. One night Albert got his hands on a baseball bat and began swinging at her, mad about something and wanting to literally crack some skulls. Karen later laughed that she was like the original Matrix the way she dodged and weaved to avoid him before some of the other boys in the house came to her defense and pulled the bat from Albert's grip. Still, she stayed—for years. She knew Albert and the rest of us were in situations none of us had asked for, that our psyches were fractured from the things we had experienced and seen. She forgave us for how we had been taught to react and tried to show us a better way. She'd say, "If you're frustrated with your mom and dad and the way you were treated, then you have to work right now on not being like that with other people."

It was a lesson in redemptive theology, something I knew nothing about as a child except through example. Janice later explained to me that redemptive theology is the notion that humans are co-redeemers with Christ. She and Ellen, and Karen too, believe that Christ came to redeem, but He wants us as His partners. The beautiful thing is, our part in healing other people is part of our own redemption and our connection to a higher power, as well as theirs.

Looking back, I see the power of redemptive theology in everything the sisters did for me and the other children. My life may have been thrown in the ocean, but when I came to shore at MacDonell's, Sister Janice and Sister Ellen and Karen and many others were mediators, there to help me go from being lost to finding purpose in my life. Whether I came to know God in the process was up to me, they all later said. Their part was getting me from point A to point B.

So in its greatest sense, redemption allowed me, and potentially all the other kids at MacDonell's, to become the person I was meant to be. It opened our hearts to a place where we could love and feel loved. And as Sister Ellen says, love is a very redemptive thing.

* * *

Karen especially tried to make life joyful for us and show us everyday love in a way our parents never had. Instead of keeping twelve rambunctious boys cooped up in the cottage when the weather was nice, we'd all jump on our bikes and head downtown with her. Sometimes we'd stop to pick flowers along the way and stick them in Karen's brimmed straw hat. The *Houma Courier* once published a picture of us all in a row on our bikes, headed for the Scarlet Scoop. Karen has kept that clipping all these years.

On weekend nights, Karen would put some Earth, Wind, and Fire or K.C. and the Sunshine Band on the record player and we'd jam out to the music. We'd tease her when Queen's "Fat-Bottomed Girls" came on, and she laughed along with us. Nobody was ashamed to dance, not even the white boys in Laskey. We secretly loved the freedom to move as a blended group, some coordinated, some not so much. It made us happy.

Karen and the sisters did everything they could to give us a life in which we didn't feel institutionalized. We were an orchestra, with Sister Janice directing us and everyone playing his or her own unique part.

* * *

But there were definitely behind-the-scenes struggles going on that none of the kids saw or realized.

The sisters were often fighting the system to give us the care we needed. At times they would go to court to prevent a child from leaving, because the alternative of sending them home or to another institution was something Sister Janice and Sister Ellen couldn't accept. State rules and mandates were changing constantly, and the changes were not always for the better. And the orphanage system was dwindling year by year, making it harder to find funding and support for our group home.

At the same time, the Sisters of Notre Dame had come to the conclusion that they would give up their work with children in orphanages. For Sister Janice and Sister Ellen, this was the hardest blow. They had a choice: to follow their calling of helping orphaned children or to abide by the direction of their order and focus on education rather than abused and abandoned kids. In the end, after a lot of heartache, they decided to leave the order.

Because the Sisters of Notre Dame had changed their focus, it made sense for Ellen and Janice to leave, but that didn't make it easy. It was the only life that either woman had ever known. Both went through the ex-cloisteration process, Ellen first and Janet a few years later. They could continue to live their vows, but they would no longer be a part of the community.

From our perspective, nothing much changed. We still called both women "Sister," they continued caring for us in the same way, and they lived the frugal life they always had, giving much of their money to charity. But for them, the lost tie must have felt profound, even though they kept in touch with the Sisters of Notre Dame community after they left it.

Their commitment to us, and hundreds of kids who followed us, remained resolute. They lived out their deep faith in redemptive theology as a way of healing broken kids, even without the order behind them. It was a testament to their belief in the power of constancy, from the way they raised us to the way they held to their calling in life.

MacDonell Children's Home

Sister Janice

Sister Ellen

The Entrepreneur

Laskey Boys

Sarah

Karen

Sister Ellen (Mom)

Group photo

Playing around

Great fishing trip

Feathering was in!

Audobon Zoo trip

Open House

San Antonio reward trip

Playing around

Boot Camp

Janice (Mom) and Paul

Savannah and Elijah

Family photo

Paul, Savannah, and Eli

Redemption

My Eyes Cleared from the Salty Tears

My eyes cleared from the salty tears
My soul aware of a time passed,
My hearts blue black chains at my feet,
My wars past choking smoke passes my lungs,
My sacred granite walls of very old,
My doomed graphite light dims,
My wretched fears scream no more,
My dreadful loneliness clears with the passing storm,
My life is new in the morning dew,
My presence warms in the light,
My heart is Open,
My spirit is Aware,
My Life is New Now,
My eyes see,
My heart feels,
My soul rejoices
Now in ALL that is True,
My Being breathes in the inhalation of Joy
and Transformation,
My,,, Ooh my How sweet is Grace!

Chapter 9

Leaving Home

When I turned sixteen, having spent half my life at Mac-Donell's, the constancy and love I grew up with allowed me to make one of the most difficult, flawed, and pivotal choices of my life. I decided to go "home" to live with my father and stepmother.

I think we are all biologically wired to seek approval from our parents. No matter where you come from or how brutal your history is with those two people, at your core you still long to connect with them and be accepted by them. For a teenage boy who had grown up surrounded by strong, supportive women, I still couldn't shake the need for a father. Knowing full well what the past had looked like and the likelihood of things turning out well, I needed to find out if a relationship with my dad was possible.

The idea started to take shape after several passable visits to see him. My friend Sarah had left MacDonell's the year we turned fourteen to go live with some long-lost relatives, and that, too, may have been an unconscious influence. I decided to talk it over with Sister Janice. True to the grace that defines her, when we first sat down she said, "Let's discuss what this means to you."

And then she listened. I offered all the pros and cons I'd been turning over in my mind. I was older. I had only two more years until graduation. He and I would be on a more level playing field as adults. Dale wouldn't be happy about it, but we could avoid each other.

Sister Janice never said, "I don't think it's a good idea." She didn't tell me the way I felt was right or wrong. Instead, she suggested I talk it over with my dad. As hard as it would be to see me go, it was clear to her that this was the choice of a young man, not a little boy.

Simon's response was typically guarded. As long as I wouldn't be a bother or a nuisance to Dale, he said, then he guessed it would be all right with him. Not exactly a ringing endorsement, but I hadn't expected him to welcome me home with open arms. As far as how Dale felt about it all, I think she found the fact that I had a pulse irritating. But I ignored that for the time being, and embraced the minor victory.

And so I went to live with my dad.

* * *

The day I left MacDonell's, the Saturday before the start of my junior year, was a beautiful southern Louisiana summer day. The ancient live oak trees on campus shone in the morning light, and the azaleas outside the cottages were in full bloom. I could smell the salty, rich smell of the intercoastal canal and Bayou Terrebonne, where I had fished and played on countless afternoons. The white two-story framed buildings I first laid eyes on that frightening day eight years before hadn't changed. But I had. I had grown into a young man here, someone who was capable of making his own decisions. They might not always be the best decisions, but they were mine.

All my things were packed and waiting by Laskey's front door. At 10:00, Simon pulled up in his green Chevy pickup. If any of the boys or counselors had been there that spring of 1973, they would have recognized it was the same truck that had brought me, Phil, and Tina to the doors of MacDonell's in the first place. And just like on that day when I was eight, I was excited, anxious, and afraid.

I invited Simon into the cottage where I had lived all my teenage years, and it stung when he declined. But I let it roll off. When he didn't step up to help carry my things to the bed of the truck, all the Laskey boys chipped in to load up my possessions. In a silent way they were saying goodbye to an older brother.

Soon the truck was loaded and it was time to go. Many of counselors were there, standing beside Sister Ellen and Sister Janice, and I hugged my closest friends and caregivers. Some of the younger boys and girls from Keener and Hooper, including my sister Tina, had quietly gathered outside their buildings too for a chance to wave good-bye. I did my best to wave to everyone as I got into the truck. But I didn't cry. I was all smiles, dogged that this moment was going to be a joyful new beginning.

James, my roommate, was the last person I linked eyes with as the truck pulled out onto the drive. I had grown up with James, and we had spent many happy days playing as young boys, as well as many lonely holidays together as two of the only kids left behind for Christmas. He was a gentle spirit. We'd made a secret pact in our last years at Laskey to work on his reading. Every night he would read to me, and we both were sure he was making progress. No one knew about our agreement because

James was so embarrassed by his poor reading skills and wanted so desperately to be in regular school classes, and I would not forsake his trust. Now he would have to find a new tutor.

As the tires rolled across the oyster-shell drive, James and I broke our locked gaze and I turned to face the road ahead. Dad stepped on the accelerator and, just like that, we pulled out onto the highway and were gone.

* * *

The trailer we returned to after our quiet drive that August afternoon was the same one in which Dale had thrown the four-pound chunk of coral at me several years before. Not surprisingly, she wasn't there to greet us when we pulled up. With no offers of help, I hustled my own stuff into the guest room that had been designated as my new room and Simon disappeared.

I spent the rest of the day unpacking my boxes and putting my clothes away, first cleaning out the dusty drawers, wiping the furniture down, vacuuming, and airing out the smoky room. Both Simon and Dale were hardcore smokers, and it was hard to exterminate the stale, heavy smell that permeated everything. But classes started that Monday at my new high school. I didn't have much time to get ready.

The first day of school, Simon drove me up to the front entrance of Thibodaux High and dropped me off. I had no idea where to go, who my teachers were, or even where to find my locker. I asked him his advice, and he just shrugged. But I was a quick study from all those years of blending in with new kids at MacDonell's, and it wasn't long before I figured out my way around.

I knew that getting involved in sports would be key to my success as the new kid. Within weeks of starting school, I tried out for football and made the team. People began to connect with my easygoing personality and my abilities as a leader, and I made new friends quickly. Before long, I'd found my niche.

One thing that helped ease me into my new situation was no longer having to live the double life I'd always lived during my years at the orphanage. Though I'd loved my MacDonell's family, I'd never gotten over the need to hide that I was an orphan from the outside world. When you're labeled "orphan," you're looked on with pity, no matter what your situation. I didn't want that pity. I was fiercely independent, and I was not anyone's charity case. So from the time I arrived at MacDonell's, my home life was a mystery to the kids at school. Only my closest friends knew where I lived, and even they didn't know much beyond that.

Now I didn't have to pretend I was a regular kid with a regular family. I finally was. My new burden was having to live in that new, single dimension.

* * *

Simon still worked the oil rigs, gone for a week to two weeks at a time, and then back for a short period before going out again. Dale still drank. That seemed to be her only profession.

Ninety percent of the time, when I was home I was alone with Dale. Although her physical abuse of me had eased off because of my size and ability to defend myself, she was still verbally abusive. The easiest way to deal with her was to steer clear of her—as much as you can in a 12-by-60-foot trailer. I buried myself in school, sports, and my new friends. After football ended, I made the basketball team, then I ran track. I tried to stay at school for as long as possible each afternoon and ride the late bus home. But when I was home, I did everything I could to smooth things over.

It was quickly apparent that my attempts at a congenial relationship with my dad, as well as with Dale, were a lost cause. In essence, I became their house servant instead. There wasn't any household task I didn't do. I washed clothes; I did dishes; I cleaned the trailer from top to bottom every Saturday. Outside maintenance was my responsibility too: cutting grass, pulling weeds, washing cars. Soon it dawned on me that this is why they had really agreed to let me come "home." They needed free labor, and someone to kick around when they weren't yelling at each other.

It was a bitter pill to swallow. I'd hoped for so much more, even though the signs had never been in my favor. Although the sisters hadn't discouraged me from going to live with Simon Sr., when I wrote to Sarah about it, I could tell she thought it was a bad idea. She had observed for years how much I wanted to be accepted by my father, and the pain and sense of abandonment I felt when he continually rejected me. Unlike any of my school friends, Sarah knew the weight of that heavy cloak.

In fact, anything that required the role of parent, Simon and Dale blew off. I'd joined the Fellowship of Christian Athletes in Thibodaux, but when the time came for the annual parents' banquet, Simon refused to go. I ended up calling Karen to ask if she would stand in as parent for me. She immediately told me it would be her honor.

That Friday night, Karen came to the trailer to pick me up. She'd never met either my dad or Dale in all those years at MacDonell's. The expression on her face as we walked out of the trailer together was puzzling. She refused to explain it then, but years later told me that one look at my dad had explained to her the mystery she never could solve. In the years since she'd left MacDonell's, Karen often told me that she had always thought I was a child any parent would be blessed to have. After seeing my father's dark complexion, his subdued and angry personality, and hearing the way he talked to me, she felt she understood why he'd left me in a children's home. This was not my biological father.

In truth, as I grew older, especially in the years after I left Thibodaux, I began to come to the same conclusion. My mother had always been gone from home a lot, even when my parents were married. She'd always had lots of boyfriends in the years after Simon left, and there were rumors that she'd been promiscuous during her marriage to him, too. When people looked at me in contrast to Phillip, Tina, Simon Jr., and Tommy, there was no question I looked different: blue-eyed, blond, and lanky where they had jet black hair, stocky, with olive-toned skin. But it wasn't just that we didn't share the same physical characteristics—our emotional characteristics didn't align either. Phil and Tina especially were fearful, withdrawn, stunted socially. And Dale had told me point blank in her alcoholic rages that I was not Dad's son. Even when I sidestepped the bluntness of her assertion, telling myself it was the liquor talking, the passion with which she hated me explained that somehow I was different, in her eyes, from the others. I couldn't bring myself to address the question directly to Simon; he was the only dad I knew.

The year I was sixteen, I was maintaining ignorance to the question of my parentage. I'd just moved in with my father, how could I accept that I wasn't actually a Buras? Karen, seeing the truth, was happy to step into the role of big sister, if not mom, by taking me bowling, to Bible study, or cheering me on from the stands of one of my games or meets. I embraced her involvement in my life, both figuratively and literally. At the bowling alley, I'd come back from making a strike and would grab her hands when she jumped up to congratulate me. She'd catch my eye, since we both knew my newfound ease with human touch was a big deal. We'd laughed when I was a boy that one day I would have a big boat and she could come sail with me, only first we'd have to tie a little boat to the back so she'd have somewhere to ride. My acceptance of her platonic expressions of affection signaled that I was ready to let her be a lifelong part of my life, to be onboard the main boat, so to speak.

Other friends besides Karen filled the gap left when neither Dad nor Dale accepted my olive branch. When my father and stepmother didn't show up for my high school graduation, it was easy to make plans with buddies for after-graduation parties. My best friend, track-mate, and confidant Byron Benoit offered an open invitation to hang out with him and his family. I loved them because they were so accepting and generous. Byron's mom even took the time to sew my football and track patches onto my letterman's jacket. When I wasn't at the Benoits' house, I could hang out with Troy Anderson, who lived up the street and had a car, and who offered me peace when I needed to escape my tiny, chokingly smoky room in the trailer. And I always had Sarah's letters to keep me company, even though now she lived in a different part of the state.

When I first arrived in Thibodaux, there was another big adjustment I had to make in addition to making new friends and navigating an uncomfortable home life. I had never been on a date. My embarrassment and secrecy about living at MacDonell's had trumped any ideas I might have had about asking a girl out to a school function. Then, as irony would have it, during my junior year I was invited to the senior prom by the captain of the cheerleading squad! Several popular and very angry football players approached me, asking what my answer would be. I took a couple of weeks to think it over. On one hand, here I was, this skinny new kid, aware of my position as an interloper among a well-established group who'd grown up together—I didn't want to ruffle any feathers. On the other, the girl in question was pretty, nice, smart, and of course, very popular. I made my choice. I would use my outgoing nature and likeability factor to win over the guys who saw it as their right to take out Melissa A. They never came around fully, but going to the prom with Melissa was a choice I was happy I made in the end.

Senior year I came into my own. I had lots of friends, lettered in football and track, and even took a couple of honors classes, something I'd never pushed myself to do before. On the day my college-prep English teacher, Mrs. Toups, read one of my essays aloud to the class, I was shocked and speechless. Secretly, I sent up a little thank you prayer to Sister Ellen for pushing me all those years in study hall. From that day forward, I was always referred to as one of the smart kids at school. I saw, maybe for the first time, that I had the aptitude to go to college.

I eventually had a steady girlfriend, Renee M, who was a free spirit, funny and outgoing. She bridged the gap between my jock friends and the nerdy academics who also welcomed me into their group. I had managed, for all the other challenges I was dealing with at home, to find a loving new family in Thibodaux.

* * *

In hindsight, those two years with Dad and Dale were a failed family experiment. If I had stayed at MacDonell's and finished out my senior year, I could have given myself more tools to go out into the world from a much healthier and calmer home base. Instead, I tried to fit into a living situation that was just as dysfunctional as before, only now I was much older.

And yet there is a lot to be said for negative energy and negative interactions. Living with Simon and Dale for those two years showed me, once and for all, that my relationship with my father was a lost cause and I could finally let it go. It also taught me to focus on the future and how I was going to escape the life that trapped them both. I had to better myself by pulling together the money so I could go to college. And so, after graduation, at age seventeen, I got my dad to sign a waiver so I could join the Navy Reserves and head off to boot camp.

Cupping fluorescent yellow green Joy

Cupping fluorescent yellow green Joy,
Cupping Wings,
Cupping giggles,
Cupping cheeks of laughter,
Cupping moonlight,
Cupping the flickering white jewels,
Cupping playful dreams,
Cupping panting breath,
Cupping oh I missed,
Cupping the essence of a child,
Cupping Happiness and Joy in Two playful hands,
Cupping dreams of glowing life,
Cupping what it is to be alive,
Cupping fireflies at five or forty five,
Cupping Joy and Freedom,
Cupping,,,,,

CHAPTER 10

Finding My Place in the World

Going back to live with Simon and Dale gave me enough energy and gumption to see that college was the choice I had to make. Bettering myself academically was the only way I could break the cycle of a life in southern Louisiana with limited job opportunities, the potential crutch of alcohol, and the kind of anger and regret I saw in my father's eyes.

But before I could apply, I had to make some money. My four-year stint with the Navy Reserves was part of the plan: the reserves would give me tuition support and professional training for the commitment of one weekend a month. I turned eighteen in boot camp in Orlando, where I spent a super-hot summer perpetually drenched in sweat. The navy's emphasis on teamwork and cooperation among a group of guys with diverse personalities and ethnicities was easy for me to adjust to—it was basically the theme of my childhood at MacDonell's. The navy's obsession with organization was a no-brainer too: I'd been a model of tidiness at the children's home, and had no problem keeping my footlocker neat, making my bed to navy specs, and keeping my appearance up to standards. That's not to say the navy didn't challenge me, it's just that I'd had years of training in figuring out institutional systems, which helped me excel at boot camp and make my time there as hassle free as possible.

As far as my placement in the navy hierarchy, I had it made. I was the athletic petty officer for my company, which afforded me a leadership position that came with a lot of privileges. One of my duties was teaching the sailors in my company how to swim. While I was at MacDonell's, I'd taken swimming lessons through the lifeguard level, so I was well trained to teach others. I helped my fellow sailors meet the other physical requirements necessary to graduate from boot camp too. Those responsibilities made the time fly by, and before I knew it, I'd graduated from boot camp and was completing my four weeks of apprenticeship training in Orlando.

That fall, I returned to southern Louisiana with a clear goal of getting a job and saving for college. First, though, I needed to get reliable transportation. I asked my dad if he'd cosign a loan on a car for me. It wasn't surprising when he said no, but it still made me mad. In his place, Sister Janice backed the loan for my used Honda Accord hatchback without a moment's hesitation. Unlike Simon, she trusted me. Karen, who taught me how to drive a stick shift in her own car, had faith in me too.

With my car and driving skills taken care of, I started to think about how I could make the most income in the least amount of time. I had never wanted to work offshore, but I knew the pay was good even if the hours were brutal. Added to that, room and board were included while you were on the oil rigs, which meant I'd spend much less money on food and rent than if I had a job in town.

In the end, I went to work for a contractor to the oil companies, a wire line service. In a lot of ways, guys who work for a wire line service are like roto-rooter technicians, only for a drill pipe instead of a drainpipe. When there's a decrease in the output of oil coming out of a well, it typically indicates a waxy buildup on the sides of the drill pipe left by the hot crude as it comes to the surface and gradually cools off. So your job is to clean out the well to get the oil flowing at full capacity again. You go from well to well, oil rig to oil rig, performing this service for all the oil companies with drilling platforms in the Gulf.

I'd work shifts of seven, fourteen, sometimes even twenty-one days at a time, with a few days to come back to shore, deposit my checks, see or call my friends, or put in my time as a reservist at Belle Chasse Naval Air Station. I'd arranged a deal to rent a room from a guy I went to church with while I was in Thibodaux. I paid him $100 a month for a place to rest my head and park my car when I wasn't offshore, and he had a once-in-a-while roommate to share his home a few days each month.

The work was extremely demanding physically. I'd finish each day exhausted, and think of the hundreds and thousands of southern Louisianans who'd done this intensely physical work their whole lives, including my own father. All of your senses were assaulted while you were on the platform. First there was the noise, from the generators roaring 24/7 to the helicopters bringing in the new shift of workers and taking out the old to the constant hammering of metal on metal. You wore earplugs to protect yourself from the noise, steel-toed boots to keep your feet from getting crushed, and hardhats and goggles in case a swinging pipe or dropped tool suddenly flew your way. We slept four to a room, ate our three meals a day in shifts in the cafeteria, and had little contact with the outside world in those days before cell phones and satellite TV. I was willing to tough it out for a few years for the money, but working offshore wasn't the life for me. I knew education was the only proven way to get myself to a different place.

I turned my focus to where I would go to school, what I would study. I knew for sure I didn't want to stay in Louisiana, so I began sending off for college information from universities in other parts of the country. I'd take the colorful brochures out to the oil rigs and study them carefully at night before I fell into an exhausted sleep. In the end I chose Middle Tennessee State University in Murfreesboro, just outside of Nashville; it was a part of the country I liked, and I could afford the tuition. I decided I'd study pre-med, aiming for a life as a doctor—something I knew would impress the hell out of my dad. Despite my need to cut all ties with him, I just couldn't shake my lifelong desire for his approval. Nearly two years from my first day on the job with the wire line service, I had enough saved to start school. I gave my notice to my boss, packed up my little Honda Accord, and headed north to Nashville.

* * *

That first year and a half of college, I lived on campus before moving to an apartment with some buddies of mine. My days and nights were devoted to studying biology, chemistry, organic chemistry, and physics to prepare myself, eventually, for the MCAT. I settled on chemistry as my major and worked hard, not only in the classroom but also at my job as an emergency room technician in one of Franklin's hospitals. My ongoing Navy Reserves work as a hospital corpsman had helped me get my foot in the door with hands-on medical training, and both my classroom work and my shifts in the emergency room every weekend were proving that I had good instincts under pressure and a bedside manner that patients could connect with.

And then, my junior year, another challenge struck, proving once again that it's not what happens to you that matters, it's your response to what happens that does. My girlfriend, Erin, came home from Student Health Services one afternoon to tell me she was pregnant.

It was a defining moment. Having lived the life of an orphaned child, and having just come off two years trying to form a relationship with my father that he unquestionably rejected, I felt I had no choice but to marry Erin and start a family. I just had to be a good dad; I simply refused to be an absentee father. This baby was going to get the love and attention I had been denied by my own family, and she would see her father as an active participant in her life.

Erin and I got married after Savannah turned one, and we moved into married student housing shortly thereafter. I added a shift at the hospital so I could work thirty-six hours every week to support my new family while I finished up my degree. In the span of that one year, my baby girl was born, I got married, earned my bachelor's degree in chemistry, took the MCATs, and applied to medical school. It was a stressful time, to say the least.

Then I was handed a gift that at the time felt like a major blow: I didn't get into med school. In retrospect, I think God was telling me to slow down and take a step back. Instead of following the advice of my advisor, who told me I should take additional chemistry courses and reapply, I reassessed my priorities. Did I want to go to med school for myself and my family, or for some other reason? Could I afford—physically, mentally, and financially—to take on years of additional schooling and a residency? In the end it came down to the fact that I didn't have to prove anything to my father by becoming a doctor. Instead, I chose nursing, and entered the nursing program at Belmont University in downtown Nashville. I started working as an ER nurse at the end of 1992 at General Hospital, and after about a year of working the night shift, moved over to St. Thomas Hospital, where I stayed for seven years.

That tumultuous time took its toll, especially on my marriage, which had never had a very strong foundation to begin with. Erin and I had been moving apart for years, and I realized when Savannah was old enough to go to school that I no longer loved my wife, and maybe never had. I tried to brainwash myself that we were doing fine, but I could see that the marriage wasn't a good thing for either of us. Finally, I moved out. And almost simultaneously, we discovered that Erin was pregnant with our son.

Everything was moving in a direction that felt out of my control. Had Erin gotten pregnant intentionally, in some last-ditch effort to keep us together? I'd never know for sure. Should I stick with the marriage when I knew it was bad for both of us? I couldn't; it was unhealthy for everyone involved. Though it hurt to admit it, I knew that the intimacy involved in marriage was more than I could handle. Unlike work, which was easy for me to manage, at home I felt untethered.

So even with Elijah on the way, Erin and I decided to split up. I insisted on sharing custody of the kids. My conviction that I would be there for my children no matter what never wavered, even when the divorce proceedings turned bitter and antagonistic.

The whole experience made me think more and more about what family meant to me. The one constant relationship through all those years—when I lived with my dad, worked offshore, went to school, got married, became a father, and started my career—had been with Sister Janice and Sister Ellen. They were my family, and I wanted them to be a part of my children's lives too. So the kids and I started taking vacations in Louisiana in order to visit the sisters. The first time we went, I told Savannah and Eli, "These ladies are your dad's moms." And I knew, deep in my heart, that it was the truth. Being with them gave me peace.

Savannah and Eli loved our time on Janice and Ellen's big piece of land just south of Houma. The five of us would go fishing or crabbing, just like old times, coming home on warm Louisiana nights to a crab boil or fish fry at their house in Montegut. Before we left Nashville I'd call up the sisters and tell them to make a list of chores they needed done, from cutting an irrigation ditch to washing the house or trimming the acre of land their house sat on. It gave them a break from the work, but it also made me feel good to contribute in a meaningful way to their lives, just as they had done to mine.

Time passed, and I met somebody new. Jennifer, my second wife, and I bought a home together and made an effort at blending our three children and creating a family together. The marriage lasted just over a year, though we were separated during the final three months. In hindsight, I saw clearly how immaturely and selfishly I'd behaved throughout the relationship.

I let my anger get the best of me, not only with Jennifer, but with the kids too. Though my first divorce had been bad enough, it was the second one that really knocked me for a loop. This second failure was a wake-up call: Somehow I kept dropping the ball when it came to intimate relationships, and I needed to figure out why. If my disconnect was from never having had an appropriate male role model or from something that happened to me in childhood, I needed to know and I needed to fix it. Now.

For years I'd avoided therapists—in fact, I'd hated them from the first time I'd ever sat across from a social worker at MacDonell's. Now it was clear to me that there was a reason: I was afraid to face my fears and my past. I had to get over that hurdle. In order to move forward, I had to get counseling and find better ways to love myself and others. I started with Savannah and Eli in family counseling, where a talented therapist taught us to talk openly with each other. I needed my kids to feel safe and comfortable around me, and the first step was learning how to communicate better with them.

Though it was hard for me to face, I realized that I had not been a kind, caring, understanding, and loving father and husband. I had hurt the people I loved because of fear and anger from my past. My behavior throughout my two marriages and divorces did not reflect the virtues of integrity, respect, and love that had been instilled in me by Sister Janice and Sister Ellen. That was about to change. The new path I devoted myself to was improving myself as a human being and a father, and becoming accountable for my own mistakes. It started with me.

Sing

Sing as your first breath,
in defiance of death,
as the pink rise,
in the purple set,
as a diamond pressed in place,
in stars twinkling in space,
as harvest glow,
in watercolors that flow,
as textured oil,
in nothing to spoil,
as the Toast,
in All of New York's boast,
as the Red Ember,
in time that surrenders,
as the spiral of unending case,
in the relentless chase,
as springs yellow daffodils,
in falls crimson red calla lilies,
as your soul fears no more,
in life's great explore,
as I adore,
Sing to me my sweet daughter,
Simply Sing,,,

CHAPTER 11

Savannah

Savannah always knew I'd grown up in a children's home. I never wanted to hide that from her, although I didn't go into the details of why I was there and what had happened to me beforehand. When she was very little, one afternoon she was watching *The Rescuers*, an old Disney video Erin and I bought for her. The little orphan girl Penny gave me a good jumping off point for explaining that I'd grown up in an orphanage too. "Does that mean your parents aren't alive?" Savannah asked. "No, they are," I answered. "I just got to grow up with a bunch of other kids and the nuns and counselors who took care of us. We had lots of good times fishing and playing and living together in a big cottage." "Oh, that sounds like fun," my little girl replied.

After the divorce, knowing there were certain things I wanted to protect Savannah from, Erin went ahead and filled in details of my childhood anyway: how my parents abandoned me, that I'd been abused, that MacDonell's wasn't always a happy place for kids. I know she embellished things I'd told her—she just couldn't get past her anger from the divorce. Savannah, being an introspective kid, watched me closely, trying to figure it all out.

What she saw sometimes fed into the stories she'd heard from my ex-wife. The divorce from Erin and later Jennifer at

107

times made me an angry man and father, and I'm ashamed to remember the bad moments when I lashed out verbally at my kids, yelling at them when I was feeling stressed out, overwhelmed, or tired from a long night at the hospital. I never hit them—all the violence I'd received from Dale and Simon made me resolute that I wouldn't physically hurt my children—but sometimes I pushed them too hard or lost patience during our weekends together.

One of my ways of bonding with my kids was to get them to toss around a football, throw Frisbee, or play catch. I loved sports, and it was hard for me to accept that it wasn't really their thing. Savannah would much rather have been curled up with a book, and Elijah liked to play alone quietly—they just didn't share my gregarious, physically active personality. I believed it was also my responsibility to expose them to new ideas, ways of thinking, and give them the tools to be successful in life. I was sure the more they were exposed to a variety of activities, the easier it would be to find one they'd like. I worked to feed their creative side—buying art supplies for Savannah, a drum set for Eli, painting and drawing with them, then hanging up their work on our big "art wall"— but I also insisted they get outdoors and be physically active. Instead of bringing us together, though, the sports aspect of our bonding time always seemed to end in disaster. When I threw the ball and Elijah flinched or Savannah dropped it, it just set me off, sometimes to the point of provoking them with angry words or names. They acted like they were terrified of me, and I just couldn't take it. "Have I ever hurt you, have I ever hit you?" I'd yell, feeling angry and guilty and frustrated all at the same time.

Savannah's reaction was to place herself between me and Elijah to try to smooth things over. She was very protective of her little brother, just like I had been with Phillip and Tina. And yet in those bad moments, I couldn't seem to see myself through their eyes: big, angry, and sometimes downright scary—the bully I'd never wanted to be. Why was I having so much trouble being the kind, compassionate father I had longed for myself?

I knew I had it in me. The kids and I had some great times together. Every year I took Savannah to see Annie, and she always dressed up in a red velvet dress, white stockings, and black patent leather shoes, looking adorable in her version of what it meant to be an orphan. To celebrate special occasions, I'd take my son and daughter to a nice restaurant, reminiscent of the Christmas dinners I'd loved so much at the children's home. But some of our best days revolved around trips to southern Louisiana, when I took Savannah and Eli to see where I'd grown up and meet the women who had made such a difference in my life.

It was a revelation for the kids to see me in that environment—especially Savannah, being so much older than her brother. At MacDonell's, I watched my twelve-year-old daughter watching me. Seeing my old home and some of the people who'd raised me made me emotional, quiet, and thoughtful. We walked under the beautiful live oaks, breathed in the rich smell of the bayou, and sat on the sidelines while the kids played tag football—just like I had done when I was Savannah's age. I could see her protective nature taking this all in, absorbing where I came from, seeing who I was deep down inside.

Sister Janice and Sister Ellen welcomed Savannah and Elijah into their home as family. It dawned on me that though my kids had all kinds of relatives on their mother's side, this was the only family of mine they'd ever met. Janice latched on immediately to Savannah's quiet, artistic side and the two of them painted porcelain figurines for hours on end. I could see she was drawing my daughter out in that special way she has with children, making her feel at ease to tell her whatever was on her mind. Ellen taught Elijah how to bait a hook and net crabs. My son's worrying nature faded away in her joking, encouraging presence.

Being with the sisters made me feel like myself again, too. They helped me show my children the man I truly was, the man I wanted them to know all the time. When my frustrated, angry side would emerge, all it took was a look from Ellen or a gentle "Paul" from Janice and I forced it down. Savannah and Elijah stared, amazed at my self-control, before running off to play.

The kids also saw my selfless side in Montegut. I tackled the chores Janice and Ellen had saved for me: cleaning the gutters, cutting the lawn, hauling topsoil to their big garden. At night we'd make pralines or do puzzles together or just sit and talk. The sisters' two dachshunds, Mickey and Moe, cracked us up in the way they mimicked their owners' personalities. Moe was laid-back like Janice, and Mickey was feisty and excitable, like Ellen. Each dog was drawn to its human opposite, just as Janice and Ellen complemented each other so perfectly. I liked that my children saw the love between these two women and the love they had for me. I wanted that for my kids, too.

* * *

Janice encouraged me after one of our visits to go to family counseling. Her quiet talks with Savannah and observations of our periodically tense interactions made it clear we had some issues to tackle. Coming from her, I began to consider therapy more seriously, as much as I hated the idea. She and Ellen remembered how I'd fought tooth and nail to avoid talking to the social workers at MacDonell's when I was a kid. My ex-wife Erin was also a counselor, and that wasn't a great selling point for therapy, considering all the hostility and anger between us. Right after the divorce, she had taken Savannah to see a kids' counselor, and I'd told Erin outright that I was against it. Savannah had begged me to come too, but I refused, feeling like Erin was manipulating me through my daughter.

Then, during my divorce from Jennifer, things hit an all-time low. I was depressed, angry, and not a person anyone in my family wanted to be around. Savannah, being the ever-protective big sister, did her best to keep Elijah and Jen's daughter, Catherine, out of my angry range. One night, toward the end of my short second marriage, Savannah, Elijah, and Jennifer, troubled by the escalation of marital discord, sat on our back porch feeling the weight of our mutual misery. "If you need to leave, Jen, it's okay, we understand," my ten-year-old son told her. "We won't feel abandoned. We love you." The courage and insight of that little boy's remarks was more than I, a forty-year-old man, had in me at the time.

When Jennifer left, Savannah, who'd moved in with us full-time at seventeen, took over. I was a wreck. I'd sit in a dark room playing sad music as loud as it would go. Savannah was clearly worried and asked me go to therapy on my own. She knew I was nose-diving, and even the family therapy we'd gone to wasn't enough to save me. I needed something more intensive— I didn't know what, but I had to work on myself from the inside out. It was clear I could no longer ignore the fears, anger, and pain that were causing my current demise. I had to take full responsibility for my poor behavior as a father, and at all costs find a way to be a better man.

* * *

My philosophy of life is that you are what you make of yourself. I've always been a big promoter of autonomy. Ellen taught me that. She taught me to think for myself, question what I didn't trust, and work hard to make my life better.

I did my best to pass that along to my children. If they had a question or didn't know what a word meant, I'd always say, "Look it up" as I offered them a dictionary. Sometimes we took special trips to the library to figure things out together. After a while, my refusal to give them an easy answer got to be a joke. They'd come to me wanting to know something or other, and before the words were even out of their mouths, I'd reply, "You know what I'm going to say."

My favorite quote, which I printed off for both my children, is this: "Persistence and determination are omnipotent." Calvin Coolidge said it, and I can quote the rest word for word. "Nothing in the world can take the place of persistence. Talent will not; nothing is more common than unsuccessful people with talent. Genius will not; unrewarded genius is almost a proverb. Education will not; the world is full of educated derelicts. Persistence and determination alone are omnipotent. The slogan 'Press on' has solved and will always solve the problems of the human race."

I believed in that, and I know it made my children stronger too, but I was beginning to see that what I could do for myself had its limits. I had persisted in trying to make things right on my own. Now I needed a different set of tools as an adult to understand and know myself, to find a way to overcome and manage the hurt and fears that had haunted me since I was a boy.

Hurt

I know You Hurt all over,
The ache of loneliness echoes nightly,
Your Heart was taken from You,
The tears find you when a moment is quiet and still,
The loss of unconditional love,
The jilting of innocence lost,
Tears roll down the cheeks when no one is looking,
A distressed gnawing soul transcends all we can mask
and hide,
To be present with no despair or sadness,
Today is Breathing.
Tomorrow is Grace.
I kneel to cry, breathe, and ask for amazing grace.

CHAPTER 12

An Angry
Edge on Life

A few snapshots in black and white flashed before my eyes. Then a longer sequence, growing, expanding. Soon a reel of images was knotted together continuously, causing me to choke with fear and struggle for my next breath.

Me on my stomach, the strong smell of a dirty flesh-colored comforter in my face. Shorts ripped down to my ankles. The punches coming repeatedly, relentlessly to the back of my head as I struggle and yell. I fight and kick with all my might, but he pushes my head down, again, into the suffocating bedclothes. I'm small, but I'm quick, high strung. I won't stop struggling, I won't, but his fist keeps pounding into me until I have no choice but to yield. Then I scream in pain as the rape begins, my little body ripped apart by this older boy, Simon Jr.'s friend, eight or nine years my senior.

It doesn't stop there. After he groans and pulls out of me, the threats begin. Tell anyone, and he'll do this again. Not a single word to anyone, or he'll find me. I nod, look around the disheveled room and capture the details. Bed, window, chair. They enter a place deep within my soul, and a dark door slams behind them.

Finally, I feel his heavy weight roll off my thin back, my scrawny legs and bleeding rectum. I move quickly: stand, pull up my shorts and lower my T-shirt, turn and run.

My legs move as fast as they can down the long dirt road that leads to our trailer. No one's home. I run to my room, slip inside the closet, lower myself to the floor. There's a blanket there, and I pull it over my head. Sobs rack my thin chest, deplete what little strength I have left. It's dark. I shiver and begin to rock, hugging myself, even though the night is warm. I've never felt so scared and alone in all my short life.

Eventually, I hear the sounds of my siblings moving through the house. Mom's gone, Dad's offshore. I get up and change my clothes, stuff the old ones into the trash. I wash my face, get a drink of water. Looking in the mirror, I steel myself. I can never say a word.

* * *

That day in counseling, I finally discovered what has always given me an edge, an angry edge on life. When I was six, I was raped by my older brother Simon's friend. He never repeated the violent act. I never told a soul. Until age forty-one, I had buried that day and the events that followed deep inside me, in a place where I thought I'd never see them again. Before, I could never figure out why certain things set me off. Why I hated being touched as a child. Why I always protected the weaker, helpless kids. What made me lash out at Savannah and Elijah, Erin and Jennifer, with angry words. I never understood what caused the big ugly inner hurt, the undertow of hateful energy. Thirty-five years later, sitting in a therapist's office seven hundred miles away from Splendora, Texas, I finally knew.

That terrible day revealed itself in my new therapist's office, the two of us sitting face to face, no one else in the room. After going to family counseling with Savannah and Eli for a little over a year, I'd realized that I needed to try something new. Our family therapist was devoted, intelligent, and a gift as far as helping my family start over. But I was still struggling personally. I needed to break through the walls of anger I'd put up around myself, quell the inner turmoil, and find peace. There was a perpetual sense of uneasiness sitting just below the surface, like a riptide in the ocean, waiting for just the right time to violently pull me down and into deep waters. I had to release it, and embrace a calmer sense of myself so I could move forward with my life.

I started looking at therapy methods that might help me address the trauma from my early childhood. Our family therapist, Sister Janice, and I all agreed that Eye Movement Desensitization and Reprocessing (EMDR) would be a good option. Reading up on it, it was clear that EMDR helped people who'd been through abuse, neglect, rape, natural disaster, or even war. The Department of Veterans Affairs used it to help soldiers coming back from Afghanistan and Iraq. If it could help them sort out painful memories, surely it could help me.

But old habits die hard. Even though I had read studies and books about EMDR and wanted it to work, I was skeptical. That old tendency to evaluate new people so I could decide whether they were worth my time and energy was still a big part of how I operated, even all those years after I'd left MacDonell's. Would this doctor be any good? Could he make a difference? I knew firsthand that all therapists are not created equal. Some are intelligent, resourceful, and know how to help their patients in effective ways. Others are middle of the road, and I had no time for that. So I showed up for my initial appointment wondering if this doctor would pass the test and be a good fit for me.

He spent our first session thoughtfully evaluating my needs, reviewing how the therapy worked, and outlining what was possible. But he also didn't pull any punches. He told me point blank that I would only get out of the therapy what I put into it. My first assignment was to write down the ten worst things that had ever happened to me. I looked at him with doubt in my eyes. "This is important work, and you need to take this seriously," he said. "Otherwise, what did you come here for?"

My research told me that EMDR is an eight-step process that begins with identifying past experiences that cause unhealthy, fearful behaviors. The idea behind EMDR is that traumatic events get frozen in your memory, so every time you recall the trauma, it's like reliving it all over again—and that can spread into other parts of your life. To overcome fear, EMDR alters the way the brain processes information. You actually create new ways of learning from your past by following prescribed steps with a therapist. Essentially, EMDR allows you to look closely at the painful event, uncouple it from the fear and emotion you associate with it, digest what happened fully, and prevent the kinds of physical reactions that normally cripple you.

The therapy's full name is Eye Movement Desensitization and Reprocessing because one of the steps to overcoming traumatic memory is being led through a series of eye movements while you recall the event. Doctors sweep their finger before your line of vision, sort of like what a hypnotist does, or they use other forms of stimulation such as taps, sounds, light bars, handheld vibration pods, or a combination to help patients dissipate the pain of the memory.

At first it seemed weird. Here I was, sitting there while my doctor told me to think about the night my brother held a gun to my father's head or the day I was abandoned at a children's home, and he was sweeping his fingers in front of my eyes. Rehashing all that pain from the past wasn't easy. But I could see it was working. I slowly worked through my list of horror, hurt, and dysfunction. Sometimes, as I released old memories, new ones—like the rap—appeared. Going to counseling was sort of like taking a flying leap into a very large cesspool. I would smear each traumatic memory across my field of vision, then painstakingly wash it from my mind and eyes. My sessions were so intense that I often didn't notice my shirt was soaked in sweat until I stepped outside into the warm Tennessee breeze.

And yet, it was transformational. In a short amount of time, those terrible scenes that had lived in my head for so long stopped having power over me. I was safe now. I was a strong, capable, adult man, not a skinny, frightened little boy. I could let the fear go. It no longer threatened me.

In the past, I had relied on humor and mockery or anger to defend myself. My own children had felt my stinging, angry words, many times. But under that armor and defense were hurt and years of pain that I refused to acknowledge or try to change. Finally, I was demolishing that pain and finding peace. I knew that I was in a period of transition that was profoundly influencing how I felt about myself and others.

Then something remarkable happened.

* * *

It's pitch black. I'm six years old again, shivering uncontrollably and crying. I rock back and forth on the cold, damp floor, trying to find comfort. In an attempt to console myself, I pull my knees closer to my chest, move rhythmically, sob. I ache all over, and nothing gives me comfort. All hope is lost. I'm not sure where I am or how I got to this dreadful, lonely place.

Suddenly, there is a strong presence at my elbow. Something or someone, without shape. I quiver, half-stepping slowly in the direction of the energy leading me by the arm.

A faint glow appears in front of us: a small, warm circle. Time loses all meaning as we creep along the dark tunnel toward the light. It's still too dark to see who is leading me down this narrow black tunnel. We eventually make it into the warm glow; it wraps itself around me and consumes my very presence. The angel gently pushes me forward into the radiance, into the brilliant light of hope.

* * *

After months of therapy, of replaying the scene of the rape and its aftermath in front of my therapist, this is the dream it eventually becomes. I call Sarah to tell her about the angel, the light, the radiance. "Have you ever told this to Sister Janice?" she asks. "No," I say. "Why?" "That's the very same dream she had," Sarah whispers. "That's the dream that led her to become a nun!"

An Angry Edge on Life

My Dance

Whimsical lilac breeze of weightless waltz,
Thick gait, congealed rotted steps of dirge,
Galloping thunder clapping in foam green fingers
upon shimmering tango,
Blustering impatience, tangled sway
of fractured stumble,
Orange-blossom breathe of sweeping meadows
tip-toeing the checkered floor,
Black chunky desperate fingers
without a grasp,
Porcelain breath, fluttering wings of chest
on Django mountain,
Craggy Trust of choked rhythm lost
as a note without a cello
White sanded warmth, jewel watered echo
in transformative still,
My hollow mask, granite eyes
of tripped over dead time lay
formless at foot,
Green mint kisses of freedom
Lemon drop laughter of heart
White aspened groves of peace
Sweetest splash of palette in endless rainbows of
laughter and love,
My fearless new partner.

Epilogue

The intermingling of my dreams, life, and redemption with Sister Janice's somehow doesn't surprise me. I know the two of us were meant to connect in a profound way, just as I was meant to know Sister Ellen and Sarah, Karen and James, and everyone else who became part of my family and contributed to making me the man I am today.

It hasn't always been an easy path. I've spent many years in therapy trying to understand the things that happened to me as a child, accept them, and let them go so I can be the person my true parents, Janice and Ellen, taught me to be. It's an ongoing and often difficult road, but I know I can get there. The words of Calvin Coolidge, that persistence and determination are omnipotent, still urge me on. Those attributes, and the love of my family and friends, are what give me strength in my darkest hours.

Though it was a terrible, damaging act, I was lucky the day my father dropped me off at MacDonell's Methodist Home for Children and drove away. It gave me what every child, no matter what his or her circumstances, should have: Safety. Protection. Love. My own parents weren't capable of giving me those things. Instead, a group of strangers embraced me and taught me what family truly means.

Because of that gift, we are bound for life. I visit Janice and Ellen as often as I can, and am honored that my children see them as their grandmas. Sarah and I talk, share, and encourage one another regularly, and we have never lost the bond that makes us brother and sister. I stay in touch with my counselors from MacDonell's, and stop by the orphanage when I'm back in Houma. For me, it's going home.

This book and my poetry are one small way I can express my love and gratitude.

Faith

I have fought the good fight
I finished the race
I kept the faith
Thank you for the honor and grace to Live
To breathe the glory of inhalation, the harmony
and peace of exhalation
To open my eyes to the vibrancy of awareness
To Feel all
Cold darkness of a black hallway I could only cry in
Warm sunshine of golden sand I could only play in
There is only One breath, One life, One true love
It is my honor this day to embrace all that I have known
and felt
To simply feel
It is here that gives me life.

This book, like my life, has been a work in progress. It is a part of my healing process, just like my ongoing therapy and the unexpected transformation I have experienced from writing poetry. I wrote my first poem one night after a moving session in Seattle with Lynn Larkin, my therapist. Releasing the hurt from my past through words felt like connecting instantly to a new friend, a friend who has become my constant companion. Poetry also facilitated a new beginning for me, as Paul Wayne instead of Paul Wayne Buras. I signed that very first poem, and every poem I wrote afterward, without my father's name, and eventually decided to legally drop Buras. Letting go of Simon symbolically through that act was a freeing experience.

The process of creating new patterns of awareness and behavior is critical to me, and writing is a big part of that. Reading is too. As part of my persistent drive to let go of my darkest fears and yield to understanding, acceptance, forgiveness, and love, I have reached out to self-help authors. Among my favorites are Miguel Ruiz, who wrote *The Four Agreements*; and Dr. Wayne Dyer, author of *Excuses Begone!*; and Byron Katie, whose The Work therapy is outlined in *Loving What Is* and *I Need Your Love—Is That True?* I have been using The Work to uncover, identify, challenge, and transform my fears to love with the help and dedication of Sue Maclaren.

My devotion to self-awareness and self-discovery using all of these tools brings me peace and offers progress I can see and believe in. The failure I have had in interpersonal relationships as an adult is directly connected to my old system of beliefs and fears. As a child I created a sense of pseudo-safety for myself by not allowing anyone to get too close. I did it out of a fear of rejection. Now I am able to move past those old ways of protecting myself and embrace trust and love.

Love is the strongest, most profound energy in this universe. Love transforms, challenges, encourages, heals, forgives, and lends hope and grace. I now have the tools to understand, accept, and love myself and others, and to embrace the life I have always dreamed of living.

It is through the love and by grace of two former nuns that I have the honor of telling this story. I believe Sister Janice and Sister Ellen are angels among us. The breadth and depth of their work offer grace, humility, and hope that we can all learn from.

* * *

There were many children who came before me at MacDonell's and many more boys and girls who followed. Their lives were just as touched by the orphanage and the people I knew there as mine was. Some of my friends at the children's home went on to live productive, full lives like me. Others were unable to heal from the damage of their early childhoods. Here are a few of our stories, and the stories of the selfless people who helped us.

Sister Janice: After leaving MacDonell's in 1977, Janice went to work as the clinical manager of the children's unit of Bayou Oaks psychiatric hospital. Today, she is a clinical social worker in private practice in Houma. She primarily works with children and families. Although she is no longer a nun, her vows are the same: helping children continues to be her calling in life. She will always find a way to give, no matter where she goes.

Sister Ellen: Ellen also went to work at Bayou Oaks, following Janice after about a year. She worked in their academic unit as a teacher. Today she continues her work with children, now one-on-one as a special-education tutor in their homes. Many of the kids she helps suffer from physical or sexual abuse as well as behavioral and psychological disorders. In her unique way, Ellen still teaches more than just math or reading. She helps damaged children connect socially to others and accept responsibility for their actions. Like Janice, Ellen has never wavered in her calling to be an advocate for children in need. Ellen and Janice, the dynamic duo, continue to serve God by giving to others.

Jerry Bridges: Mr. Bridges, who served as the president of the home, is currently retired.

Karen: After several years at MacDonell's working as a counselor, Karen left, burnt out but heart-broken about leaving. Yet even without the MacDonell's connection, Karen continued to make an investment in my life. When I was in high school in Thibodaux, we'd meet to go bowling or to Bible study, and she was always interested in what my plans were after I graduated, urging me to make something of my life. Karen worked for the state of Louisiana for many years running a job training program for low-income high school students. Today she continues her work with the less fortunate, living out her belief in redemptive theology.

Mrs. Joseph: Mrs. Joseph, one of my early counselors at Mac-Donell's, stayed on to run the kitchen at the children's home for twenty years. She always treated the children at MacDonell's as her own. Our holidays and summer vacations live on in all our memories thanks to her wonderful dinners and summer crab boils.

Shirley: Shirley, another of my counselors, still works at Mac-Donell's today. Because she didn't have children of her own, we became her family. She always chaperoned our summer field trips, going on camping trips, to the beach, riding horses, or accompanying us to many field trips throughout southern Louisiana. Despite my mistrust of people, I knew I could trust Shirley from the start.

Sarah: My sweetest and dearest sister from the time we were eight years old, Sarah and I were family before we could even acknowledge it. She left MacDonell's when she was fourteen to live with family, but we stayed in touch through letters, phone calls, and visits. Sarah, like me, saw education as her ticket out of a life of poverty and abuse, and she went to college in northern Louisiana to earn a degree in social work about the time I began working on oil rigs. I attended her wedding to Keith, her devoted husband, and have the honor of knowing their children, Katie, Lauren, and Keirsten. Over the years, Sarah and I have visited Janice and Ellen at the same time with our families, and it is always a blessing to be together.

When she was in her thirties, Sarah's biological mother became very ill. Even though she had not seen her mom since she was a very small child, Sarah decided that she would go back to take care of her and her two special needs sisters. It was a powerful testament to the lessons of love and forgiveness Janice and Ellen taught her. Both sisters were there for her during that trying time, and supported her decision to give back to a mother who had never been able to give to her.

Sarah, like me, considers the sisters to be her parents. As she says, "I am so much of who I am today because of what they gave."

James: My roommate James finished high school at South Terrebonne, fulfilling his wish to attend regular public school. Yet for the duration of his life, he struggled to hold a job. While working as a day laborer for a traveling carnival, he suffered an injury that caused a pulmonary infection, the complications of which ultimately took his life.

Robert: My other roommate, Robert, a vivacious and happy young man who was a joy to live with, struggled immensely with the pain and hurt of his childhood. He took his life on Thanksgiving Day the year he turned eighteen.

Albert: Troubled more and more as he got older, Albert eventually had to leave MacDonell's to go to reform school. Today he is in prison.

Phillip: Phillip was never able to overcome the trauma and abuse he, Tina, and I endured as children. As an adult, Phillip was hospitalized involuntarily because he became a threat to himself and others. Today, he is able to function with medication, but continues to struggle with mental health issues.

Tina: Tina stayed on at MacDonell's for several years after I left, and was always looked upon as the kind, sweet soul she truly is. After earning her GED, she got married, settled down, and had three children. She still lives in central Louisiana, and is very supportive of her family.

Savannah: My daughter and I have built a loving and stable relationship after those rocky years just before I began EMDR and The Work therapy. We talk several times a week, and see each other whenever we can. Savannah finished two years of college, majoring in theater, got married, and moved to New York City to pursue her passion to act on Broadway. She has appeared off Broadway in several productions and continues to build her career as an actress.

Several years ago, Savannah decided on her own to connect with my father. I think she needed to understand for herself who he was and what motivated him to leave three of his children in the care of strangers. When she finally spoke with him, through letters and a phone call, he told her she was the only grandchild who had ever reached out to him. He was sick, Dale had died, and Savannah could tell he was lonely and alone. As a result of their conversations, Savannah feels Simon Sr. left me and my siblings at MacDonell's because he knew we'd be better off there than with him.

Savannah continues to grow spiritually and emotionally in ways that I never thought possible. It is a delight and blessing to have such an intelligent, beautiful, gifted, and loving daughter.

Elijah: Elijah and I have made a lot of progress in our relationship. Though he has lived primarily with his mom for the last few years, this summer he is moving to Denver to live with me and finish his last year of high school. Having Elijah move in is one of the most joyous things that's ever happened to me. Elijah's maturity, wisdom, and sense of humor are gifts. They will continue to serve him well as he prepares for life, college, and the challenges of becoming a man. I finally feel I can relate to him as a clear-headed, clear-hearted father. We have laid the foundation for a kind and caring relationship based on honor, respect, and growth.

MacDonell's: MacDonell's is now under the guidance of Ms. Heidi Hillary, who has a true passion for helping children and faces many difficult challenges as the director. The children's home today houses twenty children between the ages of twelve and eighteen. Most of the kids don't stay for more than several months; none more than three years. Many of the orphans at MacDonell's today have suffered from exposure to drugs in utero and have much more violent behavioral issues than the children I grew up with.

Because the home no longer takes in younger children, as mandated by the state of Louisiana, it no longer serves as a place children six to eleven can call home, feel safe, and thrive. If this had been the case in the early 1970s, I wonder where Sarah, Hilda, Phil, Tina, and I would have gone. Dozens of young children like us are now sadly passed from one foster family to another instead of experiencing the stability MacDonell's used to offer young orphans. The children who eventually arrive there have typically been through three to five foster home placements. Those additional years of impermanence, mistrust, and, in many cases, neglect only serve to deepen the kids' hurt and build greater emotional and physical scars. Still, the children's home continues to serve its mission as best it can under state regulations, helping lost children find their place in the world. You can visit their website at *http://www.macdonellchildren.org.*

My counseling professionals:

1. Linda Arbaugh-Patin MA Lpe, Nashville, 615.373.9730

2. Dr. John Fite Ph.D, Nashville, www.drjohnfite.com

3. Lynn Larkin, MSW, LCSW, Seattle, www.transformationaltherapy.com

4. Sue Maclaren LAC, LPC, Denver, www.thework.com

Art: *The Angels* by Deborah Bridges, used for *Unremembered Wings*, www.studiobridges.com

Acknowledgments

I send light and love to all that are remembered and unremembered, written and unwritten. I am forever grateful.

Sister Janice Buescher~My Providential and Socratic mother,
Sister Ellen Baabin~ My Providential and hands on mother,
Sarah Wark~ My Sister given in grace.
Karen Hardeman-Holt~ My evangelical counselor,
Savannah Crafton, Elijah Buras~ My beautiful children,

MacDonell's staff~ William Cox, Jerry Bridges, Shirly Percy,
Marion Joseph, Stacey Williams, Jeanne Bergeron,
Sammy Castalano, Michael Guidroz.

Rick Larkin~ the master craftsman and groundskeeper at MacDonells whose friendship I still treasure.

My closest and dearest friends.
Paul Crews~ college room mate and brother for life,
Dale Koford~ wise, thoughtful, and my brother in life.

It is in Grace that we all give, live, and love,,,

Poems

3:thirty

Puddled skin,
Pitted mind,
Distant heart,
Delayed eternity,
Lost red kick-ball,
Solid red-pink
of cotton candy,
Rusted swings,
Rain twisted
and bone soaking,
Lost kite,
Soupy bitter Crackered
of Jack,
Broken bike pedal,
Fierce white Lightning,
Rolling grey-black clouds,
Ruptured balloons,
Galloping black night
of mare,
Lost uncatchable breath,
Tangled legs waking,
Sweated pores
and cold skin,
Congealed glowing fingers
of clock.
Stop,,,
It's 3:thirty again.

A Mirror

Reflecting Light and Love,
Gifting Redemptive Providence,
Raw and Naked in Truth,
Divine steps, grey concrete ascending,
Clarity, Clairvoyance, and Constancy,
Staring unwavered into eternity,
Giving your hand in Intent, Hope, and Guidance,
Brilliant Stars flickering the passage,
Compassionate Calling, crystal clear, relentless,
Blue Silver iridescent shimmers,
White golden wrist and fingers clapping thunderous
    ovations, honoring Love,
Powerful, Purposeful, Passionate Wings, Unremembered,
    healing the Tears,
Self,
Mirror,
Majestic & Amazing Grace,
Aware in Love,
Reflecting God.

Both

I loved you both,
We were inseparable roommates,
Lifemates,
Board game inductees,
My salty tears blur my vision,
Both seeking love and acceptance,
We played basketball till black,
Chased fireflies in moonlight,
Giggled as boys on a sleepover,
Joined as brothers,
Hurt by so many others,
Flying kites so high,
Swimming, fishing, exhausted, pickled and pruned,
Ice cream tipped noses,
I'm sorry,
I couldn't stop the pain,
Tears burden my sleep, wake my soul,
I fear I failed you both,
To protect, and shield,
Heaven is home now,
You're both in the grace of angels,
My Love and Acceptance are with both of you,
Robert L.,
James G.,
You are now forever safe,
      Totally accepted, and unconditionally Loved.

Canvas of Life

Coarsed linen
of breath,
Too close, ragged
  as blurred as milky water,
Delicate rainbow
  of pure expression,
Too far, cold
  as lost as time,
Gregarious splendored tapestry
  of Hope,
Unsolicited salt rolling
  as boulders of cheek,
Textured thick red popeyes
  of unwavered passion,
Masked passenger of doubt
  as loneliness of an empty room,
Blue Bird eyes
  of mislayed diamonds,
Hurdled Fear
  as swollen purple black knees,
Green meadow gaze
  of rolling thunder,
Pitted and crooked mile
  as twisted a smile,
Double Rainbow
  of palettes,

Shimmering yellow gold
  as smiles of Sunflower,
Hemp and Cotton thick
  as shadow and light,
Balanced happiness
  as uncontrolled laughter,
Stretched path
  of Grace,
Woven conscious oil thick and blinded focus lost
  in shimmer and color,
Distant fingered water of clear objective and unmatched
  clarity,
Oh canvas of life, too close too jaded,
Oh canvas of life, clear sight and awareness at arms length.
Oh Canvas.

Candles

The flickering light illuminated our smiles,
The white linen table cloths pressed to perfection,
The polished glimmer of silver and shimmer of ornate china,
The dance of the shadows upon our faces,
The grace of hope comforting our hearts,
The splendid gathering of innocence, laughing, and rejoicing,
The thousand smiles in shades of simplicity,
The hope of giving and gratitude, danced about the room
in quiet glee,
The wide-eyed innocence twinkled across their bright eyes,
The tangible hope of a better life,
The gathering of Our Sundays best,
The circle of life held us as We held our small hands
for Grace,
The honor to serve that night in illumination,
The thanksgiving that lifted us all in spirit,
We all gave thanks in gratitude in the golden dance of
warmth and acceptance,
The tall white flickering glow burned through this moment,
The life we knew was forever transformed in the dancing
flickering light of celebration of giving, living, luminous love,
in humility.

Come they told me

come they told me paaa rump a pum pumm,,,
the drum echoed in harmony,,,
the cadence tempered in rhythm,,,
my hands trembled in exicitement, and reverberation,,,
scared to focus only on my sticks,,,
smiling joyfully,, left,,right,,left,,,
come they told me,,,
rhythmic pulse of joy,,,
me and my drum,,,
nightly,, weekly,, steadfast,, determined perfection,, left,, right,,
honored to have been chosen,,,
come they told me,,,

haunting silence of familiar questions,,,
absent, abandoned answers,,,
where is my mom,,,
come they told me,,,
the play starts soon,,,
where is my mom,,,

another lossed place,,,
another missing place in time,,,
another ache of lost hope and loneliness that knows no end,,,
another hole covered in silent, damp, and cold darkness,,,
another night of lost innocence,,,
another,,,

come they told me,,,

My son

Metallic iron
  in Nare,
Salty sea
  of boy,
Playful joy
  in ice cream delight,
Thumbing numb
  as games role,
Quick shuffle
  of slide is felt,
Chuckled cheeks
  as stick of slap,
Sharp razored
  of wit,
Endless seconds
  as eternal options,
My son
  of future dare,
My Love
  as honor and glare,
Be bright and bold
  of tungsten and titanium,
My Love,
My Son,

My Vow

To Love Openly,
To Trust Inwardly,
Enraptured in vivid totality,
Firmly planted, gripped solidly,
Splashes, drenched palettes of creation,
Motherly Earth, fatherly mountains,
Rolling in greens and golds, frolicking in reds and browns,
Sweet rhythms, grace of melodies, unconditional,
Silver roped cables, mind, heart, forever bound as One,
Clear eyes on the ending,
Transparent mind of my beginning,
Live as there is only now,
Love as you have dreamed of,
Dance with no music,
Cry when the spirit overflows,
Laugh to tears, ribs aching,
Now,
Today,
Always,

This is my vow.

The True Spirit of Love

The True spirit of Love transcends the ache and loneliness
of time.
The True spirit of Love forgives moments of selfishness.
The True spirit of Love accepts jagged edges of hurt.
The True spirit of Love is the breath of Life.
The True spirit of Love is the laughter of children.
The True spirit of Love is the wrinkled smile of age.
The True spirit of Love is the hand that holds.
The True spirit of Love is the hug in tears.
The True spirit of Love Lifts the soul out of blackness.
The True spirit of Love is the first and last kiss.
The True spirit of Love is Hope.
The True spirit of Love is,,,,,,,,,

Spumoni

Dazed distant eyes,
Right, Left, paused tongue,
Greasy fingered glass,
Stunned, enamored, paused without breath,
Shiny, sparkly, silvered casing,
Thumping pulse of temple, legs listless,
Blinding Bright lights, Jars of licorice Joy,
Ugh,,,
Red, Brown, Green swirls of salivation,
Ugh,,,,,One,,,
Clacking door bell, crescendoed laughter,
Chewy cherry, crunchy pistachio, luscious chocolate,
Speechless, paused in eternity,
Hey,,,,hey kid,,,,
Cup or Cone?

Tears of a story

Prayers ripened by consciousness,
Actions matured by faith,
A crooked smile,
A fleeting nocturne,
Elegant summer dresses,
Golden spring Blossoms,
Religion at noon,
Grace to follow,
A walk of chunky acorns,
A gathering of fat pecans,
Time measured by Live Oaks,
Whispered fingers of Spanish Moss,
Captured Tormented Breath,
Cautious Tangled Trust,
Of surf and ocean,
Of bayous and spillways,
Of fragments and shadow,
We gathered as One,
One in tears,
One in hope,
One,,,

I Know Now

I know now,
I know now what hurt these boys,
I know now why they cried quietly for so long,
I know now they have lived in fear of being hurt again,
I know now their consuming fear of abandonment,
I know now tears of uncontrollable loss, being alone
and afraid,
I know now as a man they are safe and will never be left
alone to cry in the cold darkness,
I know now in grace, forgiveness, caring, and humility
they are loved.
I know now.

Whispering fold

Almond formed,
Diamond blue eyes,
Neck of nectar,
Quiet breast,
Bend of elbow,
Long lean lines of waist,
Sculpted hips,
Curve of knees,
Lavender calves,
Tapered toes,
Silky luminescent skin,
My love,
Sweet essence,
Gentle care,
Loving My Angel

Essence

Marrow of bone,
Red of Rose,
Gold of Sun
Ruby as Red,
White of cotton,
Fluffy as clouds,
Black as bean,
Green of Clover,
Purple of iris,
Brown as bark,
Gray of moss,
Silver of crosses,
Yellow as Sunflower,
Orange of fruit,
Simple as Breath,
Essence of life
and Love

About the Author

Paul Wayne, formerly Paul Wayne Buras, spent eight years at MacDonnell's Methodist Children Home in Houma, Louisiana.

After two years working offshore oil rigs and spending his weekends as a hospital corpsman in the Navy Reserves, Paul attended Middle Tennessee State University in Murfreesboro, Tennessee. He holds a bachelor's degree in chemistry, an associate's degree in nursing, and a master's with a specialty in anesthesia.

Paul fell in love with the majesty of Colorado's mountains while learning how to ski.

He now works as a nurse anesthetist in Denver, where he lives with his teenage son Elijah. He also has a daughter, Savannah, who lives in New York City.

Paul enjoys skiing, hiking, biking, fishing, photography, and writing poetry.

Connect with the author at *www.unrememberedwings.com*

Extra copies are available from Amazon.com
and *www.unrememberedwings.com*